Communicating Skills

LEVEL 8

Third Edition

Dave Martin

THOMSON

™

NELSON

Australia   Canada   Mexico   Singapore   Spain   United Kingdom   United States

CONTENTS

UNIT	WORD SKILLS	LANGUAGE SKILLS		WRITING SKILLS			STUDY SKILLS
		Punctuation and Capitalization	Grammar and Usage	Sentence Construction	Paragraph Construction	Composition Construction	
1			3 Levels of Language 4 4 Nouns Are Naming Words 5 5 Types of Nouns 6			1 Audience and Purpose 1 2 Personal Journaling 2	
2		6 When to Use Capital Letters 7 8 Using Commas in a Series 9 9 Using Commas with Dates and Addresses 10	7 Singular and Plural Nouns 8 10 Pronouns: Which Person? 11			11 Choosing First, Second, or Third Person 12	
3	12 Literary Devices: Alliteration and Onomatopoeia 13		17 Action Words: Transitive and Intransitive Verbs 19 18 Linking Verbs 20	14 Sentence Parts: The Subject 16 15 Sentence Parts: The Predicate 17 16 Varying the Subject's Position 18		13 Writing the Hard News Story 14	
4	22 Choosing Specific Nouns 25		21 Phrases and Clauses 24			19 Choosing and Exploring a Topic 21 20 Narrowing a Topic 22	23 Using the Thesaurus 26
5	26 Figurative Language: Simile, Metaphor, and Personification 29		24 Joining Words: Co-ordinating and Correlative Conjunctions 27 28 Compound Subjects and Predicates 32	25 Simple and Compound Sentences 28	27 Descriptive Writing 30		

UNITS 1–5 REVIEW p. 33

UNIT	WORD SKILLS	Punctuation and Capitalization	Grammar and Usage	Sentence Construction	Paragraph Construction	Composition Construction	STUDY SKILLS
6		32 Parentheses and Dashes 40	33 Making Subjects and Verbs Agree 41 34 Subject–Verb Agreement: Interrupting Words 42			30 Collecting Information 36	29 Internet Research 35 31 Using Graphic Organizers 38
7			38 Subject–Verb Agreement: Making Verbs Agree with Compound Subjects 46 39 Subject–Verb Agreement: When Subjects Follow the Verb 48 40 Subject–Verb Agreement: Some Special Problems 50		36 Writing the Topic Sentence 44 37 Placing the Topic Sentence 45	35 Putting Ideas in Order 43	

UNIT	WORD SKILLS	LANGUAGE SKILLS		WRITING SKILLS			STUDY SKILLS
		Punctuation and Capitalization	Grammar and Usage	Sentence Construction	Paragraph Construction	Composition Construction	
8	**43** Choosing Vivid Verbs *53*		**41** Helping Verbs *51* **42** Verb Tenses *52*		**44** Transitional Expressions *54*		
9		**47** Uses of the Colon and Semicolon *58*	**45** Active and Passive Voice *55*			**46** Writing a Business Letter *56*	
10	**48** Canadian Spelling *59*	**50** Uses of the Hyphen *62*					**49** Brushing Up on Dictionary Skills *60*
11	**51** Using Spell-Checker Software *63*		**54** Problem Verbs *68*	**52** Subordinating Conjunctions and Complex Sentences *64*	**53** Editing for Unity *66*		

UNITS 6–11 REVIEW *p. 69*

UNIT	WORD SKILLS	LANGUAGE SKILLS		WRITING SKILLS			STUDY SKILLS
12	**56** Latin Roots *72*		**55** Adjectives *71*		**57** Writing Clear Explanations *74*		
13			**58** Adverbs *75* **61** Proofreading *78*	**59** Adverb Clauses *76*	**60** Developing Paragraphs with Examples *77*		
14	**63** Greek Roots *80*		**64** Comparison of Adjectives and Adverbs *82*		**62** Developing Paragraphs with Reasons *79*		
15	**65** Other Roots *83* **67** Building Words with Prefixes *86*		**68** Pronouns *88*			**66** Persuasive Writing *84*	
16	**70** Number Prefixes *90*	**69** Using Apostrophes to Show Possession *89* **71** Further Uses of Apostrophes *92*					
17			**73** Restrictive and Non-restrictive Clauses *94* **74** Prepositions *96* **75** Making Pronouns Agree *98*	**72** Complex Sentences with Adjective Clauses *93*			
18	**76** Creating New Words with Suffixes *99*		**77** Pronoun Case *100*	**78** Combining Sentences with Prepositional Phrases *102*			

UNITS 12–18 REVIEW *p. 103*

UNIT	WORD SKILLS	LANGUAGE SKILLS		WRITING SKILLS			STUDY SKILLS
		Punctuation and Capitalization	**Grammar and Usage**	**Sentence Construction**	**Paragraph Construction**	**Composition Construction**	
19	**81** Homonyms: The Sound-Alikes *108*			**80** Sentence Problems: Fragments, Comma Splices, and Run-On Sentences *106*			**79** Using Thesaurus Software *105*
20	**83** Adding Suffixes to Words Ending in -*e 110*	**84** Using Commas with Parenthetical Expressions *111* **85** Using Commas with Appositives *112*					**82** Using a Glossary *109*
21	**88** Adding Suffixes to Words Ending in -*y 116*	**87** Punctuating Direct and Indirect Quotations *114*		**86** Using Appositives to Combine Ideas *113*			
22		**91** Using Commas with Nouns in Direct Address *120*		**89** Writing Concise Sentences *117*		**90** Narrative Writing: Dialogue *118*	
23	**93** Adding Suffixes to Words Ending in a Single Consonant *122*	**94** Writing Titles *123* **95** Further Uses of Quotation Marks *124*	**92** Pronouns: Making the Reference Clear *121*				
24	**97** Commonly Confused Words: Part 1 *126*					**96** Introducing an Essay *125* **98** Writing the Thesis Statement *128*	
25	**101** Commonly Confused Words: Part 2 *131*	**100** Using the Ellipsis *130*				**102** Writing Developmental Paragraphs *132* **103** Writing the Concluding Paragraph *134*	**99** Locating Information in a Book *129*
	UNITS 19–25 REVIEW *p. 135*						
	Mini-Thesaurus *137*						Index *140*

Exercise 1 (Composition Construction)

Audience and Purpose

Dec /08

Writing is most effective when writers begin with a clear sense of audience and purpose. **Audience** is the person or group for whom the writing is intended, and **purpose** refers to the effect the writer hopes the writing will achieve. For example, someone who writes a letter to the editor of a magazine intends it to be read both by the editor and by the people who read the magazine, and a common purpose of such a letter is to argue for or against an issue raised in an earlier edition.

Though writing has countless forms—from biographies and lyric poems to newspaper articles and recipes—there are four main types of writing, each with its own purpose. **Narrative writing** tells a story. **Descriptive writing** creates a vivid impression of a person, place, event, feeling, or idea. **Expository writing** informs or explains. **Persuasive writing** moves readers to believe something or to act in a certain way.

A. Suggest an audience and purpose for each of the following. The first one has been done for you.

1. a description of the terrain and wildlife in Newfoundland and Labrador's Gros Morne National Park:

   to help campers choose a location for their next hike or vacation

2. a comparison of two DVD players:

   To help a person who wants to buy a DVD player.

3. a biography of a local musician:

   mom helping   _For someone to learn about the life of a musician._

4. a review of the latest Spielberg film:

   to decide if the movie is worth going.

B. Choose an audience and a form of writing that would be appropriate for each of the following purposes. The first one has been done for you.

1. to convince your community to support the building of a skateboard park:

   a letter to the chairperson of the municipal/town/city council

2. to describe what it is like to be a grade eight student in your school:

   a paragraph to Amanda.

3. to persuade people to attend a play by a local theatre group:

   an article for the comirate

4. to explain how to cook scrambled eggs:

   a recipy for someone to cook eggs

5. to let people know that you have a used guitar amplifier for sale:

   an add in the newspaper

Exercise 2 (Composition Construction)

Personal Journaling

Writers do not always write for an audience; often, they keep **personal journals**. Personal journaling is first-draft, or unrevised, writing that may serve many purposes. Here are only a few reasons that writers keep journals:

1. to jot down ideas for pieces they may write later
2. to discover what they know about a topic
3. to identify what they do not know—and need to learn—about a topic
4. to record further information about a topic
5. to record sensory impressions (details about what they see, hear, smell, taste, and touch) so they can write accurately about experiences later
6. to "play around" with pieces in progress by drafting numerous titles, leads, endings, and so on
7. to learn about a topic or issue by questioning and responding to new ideas and situations

Suggestions for Getting Started

1. Create your own personal journal. (Inexpensive, coil notebooks are ideal for this purpose, but you can use an ordinary scribbler.) Write on the right-hand page only, saving the left page for any notes you might make when you later review what you have written. Date each entry, and skip a line after each entry so you can easily see where one ends and another begins.
2. Writers are seldom inspired to write. They make themselves write, and this task becomes easier when they do it regularly. Choose a time each day when you can devote a few minutes to recording ideas and information in your journal. Write about what interests you and what is important to you. This is first-draft writing, so do not concern yourself with spelling or sentence structure. The important thing is to get your ideas and impressions on paper. Journal writing is personal writing. If your journal will be read by your teacher and you write entries that you would prefer your teacher not to read, write "CONFIDENTIAL" in the margin.

A. To help you get started, respond to one or more of the following questions in your journal. Consider the "why" behind each of your responses.

- What do I keep thinking about?
- What would I like to know more about?
- What have I read, seen, heard, or felt that I can't forget?
- What would I like to forget?
- What makes me angry, sad, happy, afraid, or worried?
- What are some important things that have happened to me?
- What would I like others to know about me?
- Who is important to me?
- Whom would I most like to meet?
- Where would I most like to go?

Personal Journaling (continued)

B. Once you are comfortable writing personal entries in your journal, try recording information about what you experience:

- interesting things that people say (these will be useful later for writing dialogue)
- details about events, people, or places that stand out
- sketches of people, places, or things that catch your attention
- informal outlines for pieces in progress
- information about a topic (using your journal the way a reporter might use a notebook or tape recorder)
- words or phrases that might make interesting titles
- beginnings and endings for pieces (even pieces you have not yet written)
- details that might make interesting comparisons (which will be useful to help readers understand what you want to say)
- passages that other writers have written that impress you (making sure to record the source of each)
- new words that you discover (using them in sentences to help you remember what they mean and how they are used)

C. Try writing from a different viewpoint. Pretend to be someone else, and imagine how that person might view an experience. Write your thoughts and impressions from that viewpoint. Try several viewpoints, including nonhuman ones. This practice can be especially useful in helping you to see aspects of issues and experiences you might not ordinarily consider.

D. Once you have recorded several entries over three weeks, reread what you have written. On the blank left-hand page of your journal, jot down responses to what you have written. Consider the following questions as you respond, and focus on the "why" behind each response. Have I written something that

- surprised me?
- I really like?
- I really dislike?
- I might like to explore further?
- I might be able to use in a piece I am writing now?
- might make an interesting title?
- might make a strong lead or a strong conclusion?
- no longer seems true?
- seems more important than ever?
- really sounds like me?
- sounds like someone else?
- continues an idea I've written about before?

Levels of Language

Depending on our audience and our purpose, we use different levels of language: formal, informal, and nonstandard. There is no right or wrong language level, just language that is more appropriate or less appropriate for a particular audience and purpose. We use formal language when we write to people we do not know or when our purpose is especially important. **Formal language** does not contain slang, contractions, misspellings, or errors in grammar or mechanics.

> EXAMPLE: *business letters, essays, job applications*

We use **informal language** when we write to friends or family members. Informal language often contains slang and contractions.

> EXAMPLE: *friendly letters, personal Web pages*

We use **nonstandard language** when we speak and write to our peers. Besides slang and contractions, nonstandard language often contains invented spellings and words that have little meaning for non-peers. Speakers and writers using nonstandard language are seldom concerned about correctness.

> EXAMPLE: *dialogue, e-mails, text messages*

A. What level of language is used in the following letter? How do you know?

_____

Dear Thomas,

I am gratified that you have agreed to attend my graduation next week. As you may expect, our parents are planning to be present for this event, too, and I eagerly anticipate our being together as a family on this occasion. It is not every day that one's brother receives his high-school diploma, and I imagine we will recall the evening with fondness for many years. I am looking forward to seeing you.

Sincerely yours,

Charles

B. Rewrite the letter using a level of language that is more appropriate for the author's audience and purpose. Explain why the level of language you chose is more appropriate.

_____

_____

_____

_____

_____

Exercise 4 (Grammar and Usage)

Nouns Are Naming Words   *Jan. 27/09*

A **noun** is a word that names something. Nouns can name people, places, things, qualities, or ideas. Most nouns name objects you can actually touch or see. Other nouns represent ideas and feelings.

EXAMPLE:
people: *Vanessa, sister, lawyers*
places: *Stanley Park, Camrose, Ottawa River, Bay of Fundy*
things: *computer, apples, leg, raccoons*
ideas: *love, friendship, courage, hope, democracy, honesty*
feelings: *pride, love, fear, sadness, joy*

A. Circle the twenty-three nouns in the following paragraphs.

Did you know that Canada is the only country in the world in which you can drive a car to three oceans? Although many Canadians have visited the Pacific or the Atlantic, few have driven to the Arctic Ocean.

To make this fascinating trip, you must drive the Dempster highway, the northernmost highway in Canada and the only public road in North America to cross the Arctic Circle. Drivers should be sure to carry extra gas, spare tires, fan belts, and tools as service stations are often as far as 370 kilometres apart.

B. Add four nouns to each list.   *feb. 4/09*

1. things you might find in the kitchen, such as toaster, sink, oven:
   cup, pot, blender, toaster oven.

2. weather conditions you can feel, such as heat, wind, dampness:
   cold, wind, heat, snow.

3. qualities that a police officer should have, such as courage, dedication, intelligence:
   ~~brave~~ courage, dedication, intelligence,

4. people you might see in help wanted ads, such as secretary, machinist, janitor: *shefy.*
   machinist, Janitor, secretary, elektronik.

5. feelings you might experience while playing a sport, such as happiness, frustration, elation:
   happiness, frustration, sadnis, elation.

Exercise 5 (Grammar and Usage)

Types of Nouns

Nouns can be sorted and classified into groups. **A proper noun** names a particular person, place, or thing, and a proper noun is always capitalized.

EXAMPLE: *Sir Francis Drake, the Pacific Ocean, Redmond Junior High, Boeing 747*

A **common noun** names any member of a general group of persons, places, things, or ideas. Common nouns have capitals only when they begin a sentence.

EXAMPLE: *explorer, ocean, school, airplane*

Some common nouns, called **compound nouns**, are made up of more than one word. A totem pole, for example, is one thing even though it is named by two words. Compound nouns can take any one of three forms: separate words (*senior citizen, dial tone*), hyphenated words: (*major-general, vice-principal*), or combined words (*sidewalk, housefly*). If you are unsure which form of a compound noun to use, check your dictionary.

A. Write a corresponding proper noun beside each of these common nouns. Then write a sentence using each of your proper nouns.

1. street _Whitemud Drive_
   I whent driveing on Whitemud Drive

2. religion _Christian_
   I am a Christian

3. planet _Mars_
   My favrit planett is Mars

4. river _Alberta river_
   I whent tubing on the Alberta river

5. musician _Wolfgang Amades Mozart_
   A famis musician ib Wolfgang Amades Mozart

B. Use your dictionary to help you find the words in this list that are usually written as two separate words. Circle these words.

1. showdown
2. testpilot
3. hotrod
4. textbook
5. piecrust
6. postoffice
7. timezone
8. waistline
9. smokescreen
10. nutshell
11. lunchroom
12. bumpersticker

Exercise 6 (Punctuation and Capitalization)

When to Use Capital Letters

Some uses of capitals often cause problems. Study the following rules and examples carefully.

1. Capitalize the words north, south, east, and west only when they name regions of a country or the people who live there.

   EXAMPLE: *More than half of the world's oil comes from the **Middle East**.*
   *Our farm is just **east** of Regina.*

2. Capitalize school subjects that are the names of languages. Other school subjects are not capitalized.

   EXAMPLE: *On Friday I have tests in mathematics, history, and **French**.*

3. Capitalize the names of days, months, and holidays, but do not capitalize the seasons.

   EXAMPLE: *Last **spring** my brother decided to go to the University of British Columbia.*

4. Capitalize titles showing family relationships, such as mother, dad, grandfather, and aunt, only when the titles come before a person's name.

   EXAMPLE: *Is **Uncle** Doug's car parked in the driveway?*
   *My **aunt** is the manager of that hotel.*

5. Capitalize titles showing family relationships when they are used instead of names and used in direct address.

   EXAMPLE: *Last night **Mother** and I went to the hockey game. (used as a name)*
   *Will you be home for supper, **Dad**? (used in direct address)*

Rewrite these sentences using capital letters where needed.

1. does your aunt hannah still live in northern ontario?

   Does your Aunt Hannah still live in Northern Ontario

2. some scientists believe there may be a planet beyond pluto.

   _____

3. last summer, dad helped uncle matthew install carpets in the cornwallis hotel.

   Last summe, Dad helped Uncle Matthew install carpets in The Cornwallis hotel.

4. the german airship *hindenburg* made thirty-six flights across the atlantic before it exploded and burned in may 1937.

   _____

   _____

5. this term, my sister is studying mathematics, german, science, music, and english at queen's university in kingston.

   _____

   _____

6. on thursday, i drove kelly's mother to the library on oakland avenue.

   _____

Feb. 25/09

Exercise 7 (Grammar and Usage)

Singular and Plural Nouns

A **singular noun** names one person, place, thing, quality, or idea. A **plural noun** names more than one of these. Most singular nouns become plural by adding -s.
> EXAMPLE: *book – books   shoe – shoes   window – windows*

Singular nouns ending in -s, -ss, -zz, -x, -sh, or -ch become plural by adding -es.
> EXAMPLE: *gas – gases   kiss – kisses   buzz – buzzes   box – boxes*

Most compound nouns form their plural in the same way as other nouns.
> EXAMPLE: *checklist – checklists   jack-knife – jack-knives*

However, when the main word comes first in a compound noun, often that word is made plural.
> EXAMPLE: *son-in-law – sons-in-law   chief of staff – chiefs of staff*

A. Many nouns do not follow the simple rules above. Copy the examples below, and write in your notebook the spelling rule illustrated by each group of words.

1. a) boy – boys; way – ways; alley – alleys; monkey – monkeys

   b) baby – babies; city – cities; army – armies; penny – pennies

2. a) radio – radios; rodeo – rodeos; patio – patios; igloo – igloos

   b) hero – heroes; potato – potatoes; echo – echoes

3. a) chief – chiefs; cuff – cuffs; café – cafés; safe – safes

   b) half – halves; life – lives; leaf – leaves; knife – knives

B. Some plural nouns are the same as their singular forms. Give at least two examples of these. If you need help, check a dictionary.

_____

C. Some singular nouns, such as "woman," form their plurals in an irregular way. Give three more examples of irregular plural forms. If you need help, check a dictionary.

_____

D. Copy these singular nouns in your notebook and write the plural form after each. Use a dictionary if you are unsure of the spelling.

1. hoof	10. giraffe	19. calf
2. quiz	11. antelope	20. passer-by
3. grouse	12. galaxy	21. bus
4. volcano	13. loaf	22. scissors
5. party	14. zero	23. tornado
6. mother-in-law	15. foot	24. cupful
7. fly	16. governor general	25. chef
8. tomato	17. mosquito	26. great-aunt
9. piccolo	18. ceremony	27. bill of sale

Exercise 8 (Punctuation and Capitalization)

Using Commas in a Series

The most frequently used punctuation mark within a sentence is the **comma**. Commas are used to keep similar items from running into each other and to keep the reader from becoming confused. A **series** is composed of three or more words or groups of words listed one after the other.

> EXAMPLE: On long hikes, be sure to take a **first-aid kit**, a **pocketknife**, some **matches**, and a **map**.
> Needle-nose pliers are useful on camping trips for **moving hot pans, pulling out thorns,** and **removing fish hooks**.

A series of three items requires two commas, a series of four items requires three commas, and so on.

In these sentences, underline the words or groups of words that are part of a series. Insert commas where needed.

1. The planets Mercury Venus Mars and Jupiter are all visible without a telescope.

2. The thin atmosphere on Mercury contains helium hydrogen and oxygen.

3. An astronaut arriving on Mercury would find the surface dry extremely hot and almost airless.

4. Scientists have used radar unpiloted spacecraft and radio astronomy equipment to explore Venus.

5. The atmosphere on Venus consists primarily of carbon dioxide but also contains small amounts of nitrogen argon neon oxygen sulphur dioxide and water vapour.

6. Looking at Mars through a telescope, you would see dark patches reddish areas and white caps at the poles.

7. Plants and animals living on Earth could not survive on Mars because the surface has no water the atmosphere contains almost no oxygen and the nighttime temperatures are extremely low.

8. The four largest moons revolving around Jupiter are Ganymede Europa Callisto and Io.

9. Flights to Jupiter could send back information about the composition of its atmosphere the temperature of its interior and the life forms that might exist.

Exercise 9 (Punctuation and Capitalization)

Using Commas with Dates and Addresses

When an address is part of a sentence, use commas to separate the city from the street and to separate the province, state, or country from the rest of the sentence.

EXAMPLE: *Write to Friedrich Thiessen at 1088 West 48th Avenue, Vancouver, British Columbia V6M 2N7, for more information.*

With dates, separate the day of the month from the year with a comma. When a complete date is part of a sentence, separate the year from the rest of the sentence with a comma.

EXAMPLE: *The attack on the New York World Trade Center on September 11, 2001, altered the way North Americans view terrorism.*

A comma is not needed if the date consists of the month and year only.

EXAMPLE: *My great-grandfather came to Regina in May 1910.*

Answer each of these questions in a complete sentence. Be sure to put the commas in the correct places.

1. When will you be twenty-one? (Include the day, month, and year.)

   _____

   _____

2. Where does your best friend live? (Include the street, town or city, and province.)

   _____

   _____

3. What day, month, and year was last Sunday?

   _____

   _____

4. If you could visit any two cities in Europe or Asia, where would you go? (Include the cities and the countries.)

   _____

   _____

5. Many Canadians died in the Dieppe Raid during the Second World War. When and where did this battle take place? Use the encyclopedia or the Internet to find the answer.

   _____

   _____

Exercise 10 (Grammar and Usage)

Pronouns: Which Person?

There are three grammatical forms of pronouns that indicate **person**. In the first person, the writer is talking about himself or herself and uses the pronoun *I* or *we*.

> EXAMPLE: *I spoke to the principal about the need for new computers in the lab.*
> *We found a store that offers a discount on new computer hardware.*

In the second person, the writer is speaking directly to the reader and uses the pronoun *you*.

> EXAMPLE: *You should ask the parent–teacher association to handle fundraising.*

In the third person, the writer is writing about someone else and uses the pronouns *he, she, it, one,* or *they*.

> EXAMPLE: *They offered to hold a raffle at the next basketball game.*

It is important to consistently use the same person throughout a piece of writing. Switching from one person to another can confuse readers.

> WRONG: *We attended two computer camps at Acadia University. You really learn a lot about new video-editing techniques at those camps.*
>
> CORRECT: *We attended two computer camps at Acadia University. We really learned a lot about new video-editing techniques at those camps.*

A. Identify the grammatical person (first, second, or third) used in each sentence.

1. She began the presentation by commenting on the need for increased government funding for technology education. _____

2. I thought the discussion of technology was interesting. _____

3. One must realize that technology programs are continually changing. _____

4. You must understand that even small businesses depend on computers today. _____

5. We hope to see more technology programs introduced next spring. _____

B. The following passage should be written in the third person, but it contains switches in person. Circle the words that tell you where the point of view changes to the first person or second person. Then rewrite the paragraph in your notebook so that it is entirely in the third person.

Students who took part in computer literacy programs in elementary school are likely to be more comfortable with technology than those who did not. If we have had experience with computers in our youth, we are often more eager to use computers than are people who have not had these programs. Children are usually comfortable experimenting with computers. Perhaps this is because they are less worried than older people that they will break something. You cannot learn without making mistakes, and computers can take a lot of punishment.

Exercise 11 (Composition Construction)

Choosing First, Second, or Third Person

One of the most important decisions a writer makes when writing a piece is the grammatical **person** in which the piece is written. The various persons shape what the writer will share and how the reader will respond to it. Writing in the first person emphasizes the writer because it is personal, so it works well when writing informal letters and pieces based on personal experience.

> EXAMPLE: *My most embarrassing moment occurred in grade seven when I walked into the wrong change room by mistake.*

Using the second person emphasizes the reader, so it is useful when the writer wants to give instructions or advice.

> EXAMPLE: *To make the best pancakes, you must be careful not to stir the batter too much.*

The third person emphasizes the subject, so it is appropriate to use when writing reports.

> EXAMPLE: *Fire department officials stated that the cause of the fire was arson.*

A. Suggest the most appropriate person for each of the following pieces of writing, and give a reason for your choice.

1. an operator's manual for a DVD player _____

   _____

2. an explanation of asthma _____

   _____

3. an account of a favourite vacation experience _____

   _____

4. a comparison of the best universities in Canada _____

   _____

B. Choose one of the following situations and write a first-person account of the event in your notebook.

- your first day of school
- your first ride on a roller coaster
- your most frightening experience
- your happiest memory
- your most memorable class trip
- your first trip to the hospital

C. Rewrite your account above using the third person. Read both aloud, and tell which you prefer and why.

Exercise 12 (Word Skills)

Literary Devices: Alliteration and Onomatopoeia

Writers often use techniques that appeal to the sense of sound to catch their readers' interest and to emphasize certain impressions. One technique, **alliteration**, is the use of words that begin with similar sounds. Repeating soft sounds such as *l* or *m* can help create a feeling of peace and tranquility.

EXAMPLE: *The lilting lullaby lulled us to sleep.*

Repeating hard sounds such as *d* or *k* can help generate a feeling of action, excitement, or tension.

EXAMPLE: *A dark figure darted into the doorway.*

Onomatopoeia is the use of words that imitate sounds, which can heighten the vividness of a written experience.

EXAMPLE: *bang, boom, clatter, crash*

UNIT 3

A. In the blanks tell whether the writer used alliteration or onomatopoeia in each of these sentences, and describe the effect intended.

1. Waves lapped at the side of the canoe. _____

_____

2. Basketballs battered the backboard during practice. _____

_____

3. The apple crunched as Kyle bit into it. _____

_____

4. The soothing sounds of the sea smoothed the worry from her face. _____

_____

B. Newspaper headlines often use alliteration to catch readers' interest while introducing the main idea of a news story. Browse through some newspapers and copy in your notebook five headlines that use alliteration. Tell whether each is successful in catching the readers' interest and introducing the main idea of the story.

C. List at least three onomatopoeic words that are associated with each of the following locations:

1. a school bus _____

2. an office _____

3. a restaurant _____

Writing the Hard News Story

Newspapers include many forms of writing, but many readers consider the **hard news story** to be the most important. Hard news refers to stories written about events that are happening now. Most hard news stories have the following features:

- The headline announces the content of the story concisely and catches readers' interest.
- Often, the place where the event occurred is stated in block letters at the beginning of the story.
- The first one or two paragraphs answer the questions *who, what, when, where, why,* and *how.*
- The writer writes in the third person, presenting only the facts associated with the event, not his or her personal feelings about it. If the story includes opinions, they are presented as quotations from people who are involved in some way with the event.
- The writer establishes the identity of every person mentioned in the story by clarifying his or her role in the event.
- The writer arranges information about the event from most to least important. (This makes it easy for editors to shorten a story to fit the space available on the page.)
- To make narrow newspaper columns easy to read, paragraphs are short, seldom longer than two or three sentences.

Gas guzzler grounds thieves

RATHBURNE — A month-long series of robberies in the Rathburne area ended Friday night when police arrested two men shortly after an attempted break-and-enter at Kroeger's Gas Bar on Water Street.

Karl Taylor, 27, and Shawn Brickton, 25, were apprehended after their vehicle ran out of gas during a high-speed chase on Highway 104.

Police were called to the scene when owner Jack Kroeger pressed an alarm wired to the Rathburne Police Station.

"I was in the back office working late on payroll when I heard someone trying to get in," Kroeger said. "The place was locked up and they didn't know I was there."

Kroeger said the men fled when they heard the police sirens. Fortunately for Kroeger, police were only a block away when the call came in.

"We were there in less than a minute," Constable Cheryl Danforth explained, "just in time to see the suspects' vehicle roar off." Danforth and her partner, Constable Ryan Greer, initiated a high-speed chase, which lasted only ten minutes before the vehicle, a 2001 Ford Explorer, ran out of fuel.

Although the pair was interrupted before entering the gas bar, a search of the vehicle yielded items taken in several other robberies over the past four weeks. Stolen property ranged from cash and jewellery to stereo equipment and digital cameras.

Police have been looking for the thieves for weeks, but until now the pair have entered and escaped undetected. Previous leads yielded no suspects.

"Lucky for me those SUVs burn a lot of gas," commented Kroeger. "I'm glad they didn't decide to fill up beforehand."

Writing the Hard News Story (continued)

A. Read the hard news story "Gas guzzler grounds thieves" and tell whether it has each of the features listed on the opposite page. Give examples to show what you mean.

_____

_____

_____

_____

_____

_____

_____

_____

_____

_____

_____

_____

_____

_____

_____

B. Find two hard news stories in different newspapers that report on the same event. (Use the Internet if your community does not have two newspapers.) Clip and paste them neatly in a folder. Then read each story carefully and explain whether you think the two newspapers reported the event in much the same way. Give examples from each story to support your ideas.

C. Choose a real event in your community that you can research. (You may want to base your story on a recent event or on one that happened in the past.) In your journal, collect information about the event from as many people as possible, making sure to record where you got the information.

D. Use the information you collected to write a hard news story that has the same features you have learned. If possible, use a word-processing program to present it in newspaper format.

Exercise 14 (Sentence Construction)

Sentence Parts: The Subject

A **sentence** is a group of words that makes sense by itself. Every sentence has two basic parts: a subject and a predicate. All the words that tell who or what the sentence is about are called the **complete subject**.

> EXAMPLE: **The small black box near the fireplace** exploded suddenly.

The complete subject always has a key word that clearly answers the following questions: Who or what is doing this action? Who or what is this sentence about? This key word is called the **simple subject**. In the example above it was the box that exploded. The word *box*, therefore, is the simple subject.

A complete subject and a simple subject can be the same thing.

> EXAMPLE: **Elephants** are extremely strong and very intelligent.

A. Underline the complete subject in each sentence. Circle the simple subject.

1. The storm last Wednesday flooded several subdivisions near Winnipeg.

2. The huge hailstones damaged the greenhouses.

3. Joseph-Armand Bombardier invented the snowmobile in 1922.

4. Many farmers in southern Alberta raise beef cattle.

5. The truck beside the barn belongs to Uncle Mark.

6. The candle on the table sputtered and went out.

7. The family of otters slid down the bank and into the pond.

8. The mushrooms under those trees are poisonous.

9. The house across the street burned down yesterday.

10. The skin of an African elephant weighs almost a tonne.

B. Write four sentences of your own and circle the complete subject in each.

1. _____

_____

2. _____

_____

3. _____

_____

4. _____

_____

Exercise 15 (Sentence Construction)

Sentence Parts: The Predicate

Every sentence has two basic parts: a subject and a predicate. All the words that tell who or what the sentence is about are called the complete subject. All the words that tell what the subject does are called the **complete predicate**.

EXAMPLE: My uncle in Germany *sent me those stamps*.

Within each complete predicate, a key word or phrase tells what the subject does. This main word or phrase is called the **simple predicate**, or **verb**. Without a verb, a group of words cannot be a sentence. Usually verbs are action words that tell what the subject does.

EXAMPLE: The two prairie dogs **watched** the coyote intently.

Sometimes verbs explain what is happening in someone's mind.

EXAMPLE: For centuries people **dreamed** about going to the moon.

Sometimes the complete predicate and the simple predicate are the same.

EXAMPLE: The old man **wept**.

Verbs can also help us understand what something is, was, or will be.

EXAMPLE: My brothers **are** soccer fans.

Underline the complete predicate in each sentence. Circle the action verb (the action word) that is the simple predicate.

EXAMPLE: French soldiers (built) the fortress of Louisbourg on Cape Breton Island.

1. They located the fort here to guard the entrance to the St. Lawrence River.

2. Louisbourg grew quickly. More than one thousand people lived there within a few years.

3. Ships from France arrived each year to haul away tonnes of dried fish.

4. French soldiers erected enormous walls around Louisbourg for protection in the early 1740s.

5. War began between France and Britain in 1744.

6. A fleet of more than one hundred British ships attacked Louisbourg on April 30, 1745.

7. The fortress surrendered six weeks later.

8. The British government returned Louisbourg to the French in 1748.

9. Britain and France resumed their war in 1755.

10. British troops under Major General Amherst destroyed Louisbourg three years later.

Exercise 16 (Sentence Construction)

Varying the Subject's Position

Usually the subject is at the beginning of the sentence. When the subject comes before the verb, a sentence is said to be in **natural order**.

EXAMPLE: **A colony of sea lions** lives on those islands.

Always putting the subject first can make your writing seem dull and repetitious. To add interest, try moving the subject to the end of some of your sentences. A sentence in which the predicate comes before the subject is said to be in **inverted order**.

EXAMPLE: On those islands lives **a colony of sea lions**.

Often the subject can be placed in the middle of the predicate. This is called **split sentence order**.

EXAMPLE: On June 4, 1838, **two teams from Ontario** played Canada's first recorded baseball game.

A. Underline the complete subject in each sentence.

1. In 1874 the Guelph Maple Leafs won the world's semi-pro baseball championship in Waterton, New York.

2. For the opening of the 1914 baseball season in Saskatoon, most storekeepers closed their shops for the day.

3. In Kamloops, British Columbia, an eclipse of the sun delayed an early baseball game.

4. During his major league career, pitcher Fergie Jenkins from Chatham, Ontario, won almost three hundred games. Four times Jenkins won the award as Canada's male athlete of the year.

5. As a member of the Montreal Royals in 1946, Jackie Robinson became the first black player in "organized" baseball.

6. In 1983 the Canadian Baseball Hall of Fame and Museum was established.

7. During their first four years in the American League, the Toronto Blue Jays attracted more than six million fans.

B. Rewrite these sentences in inverted or split sentence order.

1. The herd of mountain sheep grazed beside the highway.

_____

_____

2. A killer whale's skeleton lay on the rocks at the base of the cliff.

_____

_____

Exercise 17 (Grammar and Usage)

Action Words: Transitive and Intransitive Verbs

Most **verbs** are action words.

EXAMPLE: *Our high-school basketball team* **won** *the district championship.*

Action verbs come in two kinds: transitive and intransitive. A **transitive verb** needs a noun phrase, called a **direct object**, to complete its meaning. A direct object receives the action of the verb. You can identify the direct object by asking the question Whom? or What? after the verb.

In the example above, "the district championship" is the direct object of the transitive verb "won" because it answers the question "Won what?"

Some action verbs do not need a direct object to complete their meaning. These verbs are called **intransitive verbs**.

EXAMPLE: *Gerri* **laughed** *for several minutes.*

Depending on how they are used, some verbs may be either transitive or intransitive.

EXAMPLE: *The hockey player* **scored** *a goal. (transitive verb)*
Jenna **scored** *in every one of the team's games. (intransitive verb)*

A. Circle the verb in each of the following sentences. In the blank write "T" if it is used as a transitive verb or "INT" if it is used as an intransitive verb.

_____ 1. Carmelita fumbled through her pockets for a cough drop.

_____ 2. The librarian thanked the students for their help after the flood.

_____ 3. Before the assembly, our teacher explained the rules of the student council election.

_____ 4. At the end of the race, I flopped wearily onto the grass.

_____ 5. Several teenagers in our area built a skateboard park near the river.

B. Use each of the following action verbs in two sentences. In the first sentence use it as a transitive verb. In the second sentence use it as an intransitive verb.

1. ran _____

_____

2. shouted _____

_____

3. jumped _____

_____

4. clapped _____

_____

Exercise 18 (Grammar and Usage)

Linking Verbs

Not all verbs are action words. Verbs that do not show action are called **state of being verbs**, or **linking verbs**. These verbs make statements about a subject. A linking verb connects the subject with another word in the sentence that either renames or describes the subject.

> EXAMPLE: *The woman in the grey suit **is** my aunt.* (renames the subject)
> *Ranjit **was** nervous during the competition.* (describes the subject)

Many linking verbs are forms of the verb *to be*. Some of the most common forms of this verb are *is, am, are, was, were, may be, should be, would be,* and *could have been*. However, there are other linking verbs, such as the following: *appear, become, feel, grow, look, remain, seem, smell, sound, stay, taste, turn*.

> EXAMPLE: *That milk **smells** sour to me.* (The word *sour* describes the subject.)
> *John Turner **became** prime minister of Canada in 1984.* (The words *prime minister* rename the subject.)

Underline the linking verb in each sentence. Then circle the two words that the verb links. The first word you circle will be the simple subject. The second word must either rename or describe the subject.

EXAMPLE: The most important (crop) grown in southern Manitoba is (wheat)

1. George Stephen was the first president of the Canadian Pacific Railway.

2. The small snake appeared harmless.

3. The Mi'kmaq were the first inhabitants of Prince Edward Island.

4. The provincial flower of Ontario is the white trillium.

5. The car looked purple under the streetlights.

6. The surface of that table feels smooth.

7. Marco should be the winner.

8. The Okanagan Valley is one of the most important agricultural regions in British Columbia.

9. The curtains from the boxes in the attic smelled musty.

10. About ten o'clock the weather turned cold.

11. The weather in Whitehorse has been sunny.

12. That pronunciation sounds correct.

13. Blue litmus paper turns red in an acid.

14. Saskatoon is the second largest city in Saskatchewan.

Exercise 19 (Composition Construction)

Choosing and Exploring a Topic

Sometimes writers are assigned topics to write about, and sometimes they get to choose their own. In either case, writers know they write best when they write about what they know and what interests them. If they do not know enough about a topic, they either discard it or learn more about it so they can write about it knowledgeably. Before they begin, however, they make sure they have a strong sense of their audience and purpose, and they decide whether to write in first, second, or third person.

A. Identify the audience and purpose of your piece of writing. Are you writing for your teacher, your peers, a family member, a person in your community, an organization, etc.? Will you give an account of an event, describe a person or experience, provide information, or persuade your audience to believe something or act in a certain way? What grammatical person would be best to use in this piece? State your audience, purpose, and person below.

UNIT
4

_____

_____

B. If you have the opportunity to choose your own topic, read over your journal to see the kinds of things you have written about recently. Respond to what you have written by following some of the suggestions listed in Activity D in Exercise 2. Record some of your ideas below.

_____

_____

_____

_____

_____

C. Once you have identified some possible topics, put check marks beside those that interest you most. From these, choose one you think you could write about effectively. Is it suitable for your audience and purpose? If so, write it below. If not, choose another.

_____

Exercise 20 (Composition Construction)

Narrowing a Topic

Once you have a topic you are comfortable writing about, check to see whether your subject should be **narrowed**, or **limited**. The more specific the subject, the more interesting and informative your writing will be. Let's see how a broad topic such as *animals* would be narrowed to a subject suitable for a paragraph.

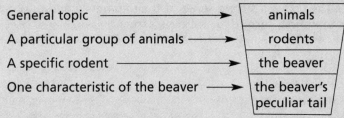

General topic ⟶ animals

A particular group of animals ⟶ rodents

A specific rodent ⟶ the beaver

One characteristic of the beaver ⟶ the beaver's peculiar tail

Here is an example of a paragraph using the narrowed topic "the beaver's peculiar tail." Notice how all the sentences in the paragraph are about this main idea.

Probably the most outstanding characteristic of the beaver is its flat, paddle-shaped tail. This tail is covered with black, scaly skin. In the water the tail acts as a rudder, allowing the beaver to change direction by shifting the angle of its tail. On land it becomes a prop, supporting the beaver as it stands on its hind legs to feed or work. The tail is also used to slap the water sharply just before the animal dives below the surface. This loud whack is a signal to other beavers in the area that danger is near. Within seconds they will all disappear.

A. Following each of the broad topics printed in boldface type is a set of related topics. In each set, three of the topics are too general to be used as the subject of a six- to ten-sentence paragraph. Underline the two remaining topics that would make good paragraphs.

EXAMPLE: **Birds**
    a. Birds of North America
    b. Teaching a budgie to talk
    c. Bird migration
    d. How birds communicate
    e. Why ostriches can't fly

1. **Hobbies**
   a. Coin collecting
   b. Buying a stamp album
   c. Launching a model rocket
   d. Photography
   e. Model railroads

2. **The Human Body**
   a. The digestive system
   b. The five senses
   c. The heart as a pump
   d. The body's muscles
   e. How the liver purifies blood.

3. **Dogs**
   a. Training a dog
   b. Housetraining a pup
   c. Kinds of dogs
   d. Building a dog house
   e. Caring for your dog

Narrowing a Topic (continued)

B. Listed below in boldface type are some general subjects. Narrow each topic to one that is suitable for an interesting paragraph of six to ten sentences. Try to choose subjects you find intriguing, because writing about topics that interest you is always easier and more enjoyable. Within each set be sure each topic is more specific than the one preceding it.

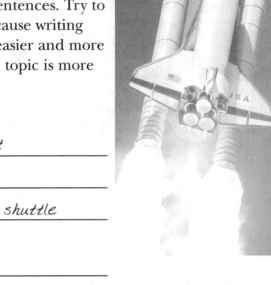

EXAMPLE: **Space travel**

    a. *types of spacecraft*

    b. *the space shuttle*

    c. *uses of the space shuttle*

1. **Physical fitness**

    a. _____

    b. _____

    c. _____

2. **Chores**

    a. _____

    b. _____

    c. _____

3. **My school**

    a. _____

    b. _____

    c. _____

C. Write your own general topic below and then narrow it.

_____

_____

_____

_____

UNIT
4

Exercise 21 (Grammar and Usage)

Phrases and Clauses

A **phrase** is a group of words that lacks a verb, a subject, or both, and functions as a single unit in a sentence.

EXAMPLE: *the angry child* (lacks a verb)
kicked and screamed (lacks a subject)
red and gold (lacks both a subject and a verb)

A **clause** is a group of words that contains both a verb and its subject. An **independent clause** (or **main clause**) makes a complete thought and can stand alone as a sentence. A **dependent clause** (or **subordinate clause**) cannot stand alone as a sentence.

EXAMPLE: *we walked to the mall* (independent clause)
when the rain ended (dependent clause)

Read each of the following groups of words carefully and tell whether each is a phrase (P), an independent clause (I), or a dependent clause (D). Be prepared to tell how you know.

1. none of the students _____

2. people cheered _____

3. when the teacher came back _____

4. because Sherry was angry _____

5. after the Halloween dance _____

6. pulling on one end of the rope _____

7. please come here _____

8. after we ate our lunch in the cafeteria _____

9. before the movie ended _____

10. all alone in the dark _____

11. beyond the edge of the forest _____

12. rats moved inside the garbage can _____

13. running in the race on the long weekend _____

14. because he was upset _____

15. after everyone had settled down _____

16. open this bottle _____

17. lifting the television into our van _____

18. as he opened the large brown envelope _____

Exercise 22 (Word Skills)

Choosing Specific Nouns

General nouns refer to a group or category of people, places, or things; **specific nouns** refer to only one member of that group.

EXAMPLE: *home* (general noun)
   apartment, condominium, bungalow, duplex (specific nouns)

Using specific nouns adds interest and vitality to writing because they help readers see exactly what the writer intends. When you revise your writing, try to replace general nouns with more specific nouns.

A. Write at least three specific nouns for each of these general nouns.

1. desert _____

2. colour _____

3. flower _____

4. fish _____

5. candy _____

6. sport _____

7. holiday _____

8. actor _____

B. Rewrite the following sentences, substituting a specific noun for each italicized word or group of words.

EXAMPLE: Is *that building* the tallest in *the city?*

   Is the Royal Centre the tallest building in Vancouver?

1. *The man* sold *vegetables* in *the park.*

   _____

2. *That girl* is an excellent *musician.*

   _____

3. While I studied, *my friend* watched *a television program.*

   _____

4. Who owns *the red car* parked in front of *the restaurant?*

   _____

C. In your notebook write five sentences describing your bedroom. Use specific nouns.

UNIT
4

Exercise 23 (Study Skills)

Using the Thesaurus

Effective writers avoid repetition by using a variety of words that keep their writing fresh and interesting. To broaden their vocabulary, writers read a lot. They also use reference books such as a **thesaurus**, which is a collection of synonyms—words that have similar meanings—and antonyms—words that are opposite in meaning.

EXAMPLE: *progress: advance, proceed, move ahead; antonym: regress*

The entries in a thesaurus may be arranged in various ways. One type of thesaurus arranges entries alphabetically, like a dictionary, and each word is followed by synonyms and antonyms. Another type of thesaurus lists words alphabetically in an index; these words are followed by numbers that identify where in the thesaurus to find their synonyms and antonyms. Most thesauri will identify the part of speech of each word listed, and this will help you decide which synonyms or antonyms are more suitable for your purpose. However, it is important to use a dictionary when using a thesaurus, because not all synonyms or antonyms are appropriate for all situations.

A. Imagine that you want to replace the word *drive* with a synonym in the following sentence: *Sarah went for a drive this afternoon.* One thesaurus lists the following synonyms: *expedition, journey, outing, trip.* Which synonym is most suitable for this sentence? Why?

_____

_____

B. The word *group* has many synonyms. Use a thesaurus and a dictionary to help you identify the most suitable synonym for the following uses:

1. a *group* of lions _____

2. a *group* of fish _____

3. a *group* of birds _____

4. a *group* of whales _____

5. a *group* of snakes _____

6. a *group* of elephants _____

C. Create a personal thesaurus by making a separate section in your journal where you can list interesting and useful words that you encounter as you read and write. Make separate categories such as specific nouns, vivid verbs, and words that describe, and write sentences using them so you will understand their exact meaning. Try to add two words to each category every week.

Exercise 24 (Grammar and Usage)

Joining Words: Co-ordinating and Correlative Conjunctions

A **conjunction** is a word that connects words or groups of words. There are three kinds of conjunctions: co-ordinating, correlative, and subordinating. You will learn about subordinating conjunctions in Exercise 52.

Co-ordinating conjunctions join single words or groups of words that have equal importance. There are seven co-ordinating conjunctions: *and, or, nor, for, but, so,* and *yet.*

EXAMPLE: Two minerals mined in Manitoba are **nickel** and **copper**. (two nouns)
The fans **shouted** and **stamped** their feet. (two verbs)
The rope was **thin** but **strong**. (two adjectives)
The cougar moved **quickly** yet **carefully** through the tall grass. (two adverbs)

Correlative conjunctions always come in pairs. They *correlate* or "show the connection between" two parallel or similar parts of a sentence. The most common correlative conjunctions are *both/and, either/or, neither/nor, not/but,* and *not only/but also.*

EXAMPLE: Last winter my sister visited **both** Antigua **and** Martinique.
Either Antonio **or** Steven will sing.

A. Circle the co-ordinating or correlative conjunctions in these sentences. On the line below each sentence, tell which words are joined and whether the conjunctions are co-ordinating or correlative.

EXAMPLE: Only an expert could tell whether the pearls were valuable or worthless.

valuable, worthless   *co-ordinating conjunction*

1. Large spiders sometimes eat tadpoles or small fish.

2. Neither Samantha nor her brother knew the answer.

3. The exhausted marathon runner staggered and collapsed six metres from the finish line.

4. There's room in the back seat for both Noriko and her sister.

5. The investigators searched the wreckage of the plane quickly but thoroughly.

B. Write interesting sentences in your notebook, following these directions.

1. Use *both/and* to connect two proper nouns.

2. Use *yet* to connect two adverbs.

3. Use *either/or* to connect two verbs.

4. Use *not only/but also* to connect two nouns.

5. Use *but* to connect two adjectives.

Exercise 25 (Sentence Construction)

Simple and Compound Sentences

A **simple sentence** has only one subject and one predicate.
> EXAMPLE: My cousin Tracey scored the most baskets during the game.
>   subject   predicate

A **compound sentence** is made up of two or more simple sentences joined by a co-ordinating conjunction. Note that a comma is used before the conjunction.
> EXAMPLE: **Mr. Harrison marked our tests,** and **he will return them today.**

To add interest to your writing, try joining some of your simple sentences with co-ordinating conjunctions. When you write a compound sentence, be sure both parts belong together. Use *and* when the second sentence gives additional information.
> EXAMPLE: The wind dropped, **and** the sea became calm.

Use *but* when the second sentence gives an opposite or different idea.
> EXAMPLE: Emily enjoys science, **but** Tejinder prefers history.

Use *or* when the second sentence gives a choice.
> EXAMPLE: Turn the stereo down, **or** my neighbour will complain.

Using too many compound sentences is just as ineffective as using too many simple sentences. Be careful not to overuse either form. Mixing different kinds of sentences will make your writing livelier and more interesting.

A. Rewrite each of the following sentence pairs as a compound sentence. Use the conjunctions *and*, *but*, or *or*.

1. I finished the project. Luke took all the credit.

   _____

2. The weather must improve soon. The plane will be unable to take off.

   _____

3. A bat is well suited to life in the air. It is virtually helpless on the ground.

   _____

4. In a flash the hungry piranhas swarmed around the helpless deer. Within minutes only a skeleton remained.

   _____

   _____

B. In your notebook add a suitable simple sentence of your own to make each of the following word groups into a compound sentence. Be sure the two parts of the sentence are closely related.

1. I enjoy watching football on television, but
2. The car skidded out of control, and
3. Don't connect those two wires, or
4. The students built a huge bonfire, and
5. Leave that dog alone, or

Exercise 26 (Word Skills)

Figurative Language: Simile, Metaphor, and Personification

Writers often use comparisons to help readers understand the person, thing, idea, or situation being described. *Figurative language* is a literary device that makes comparisons that are not literal. Three types of figurative comparisons are simile, metaphor, and personification. A **simile** is a direct comparison using *like* or *as*.

EXAMPLE: Kirk felt **as light as air** as he walked across the stage to accept his trophy.

A **metaphor** is an implied comparison that requires the reader to participate in making the comparison by mentally associating one image with another image. Metaphor makes use of specific nouns and vivid verbs to generate the comparison.

EXAMPLE: The principal **flew** down the hallway.

Personification is a special kind of comparison in which an animal, inanimate object, or idea is given human qualities.

EXAMPLE: The thought **nagged** at him all morning.

A. In your notebook explain the comparison made in each sentence, and identify the type of comparison the writer has used.

1. Relief washed over Alex as he looked at the test paper.

2. Natasha felt like she had won the lottery when she learned about the job offer.

3. The warm breeze drew pictures on the lake.

4. The mountain stood guard over the valley.

5. The night was a cold, wet blanket of loneliness.

B. In the blanks below write sentences using figurative comparisons that convey strong impressions of each of the following situations. (Be sure to think of comparisons that appeal to more than just the sense of sight.) Create at least one example each of simile, metaphor, and personification. Identify the type of comparison you have created in each.

1. a crowded movie theatre _____

_____

2. a cemetery at night _____

_____

3. a swimming pool on a hot summer day _____

_____

4. a field or park covered with new-fallen snow _____

_____

5. a litter-filled gutter _____

_____

UNIT 5

Exercise 27 (Paragraph Construction)

Descriptive Writing

Effective **descriptive writing** conveys a specific impression of a person, place, object, event, or idea. Though a strong description usually includes physical details of its subject, it often includes words, images, and details that appeal to more than one sense. Descriptive writing makes use of figurative language that paints vivid mental images and helps establish the overall mood of the passage, which is the feeling the passage creates in the reader.

Word choice is extremely important in helping create a particular mood because words have connotations that convey different impressions. **Denotation** means the most specific or direct meaning of a word; **connotation** refers to the ideas that readers associate with that word. For example, both *slow* and *poky* have similar denotations, but poky has a more negative connotation.

The more details a description includes, the better a reader is able to see, hear, feel, smell, or taste what the writer is describing. Writers take care to arrange their details in an order that readers can easily follow. They may arrange their details spatially (e.g., from near to far, from left to right, or from top to bottom), or chronologically (e.g., from first to last), or they may use a variety of other arrangements.

A. Below are two brief descriptions of the same subject. Read each passage at least twice and identify its mood. Explain how the writer creates this mood.

1. The old cemetery lay silent and still beneath a soft blanket of fresh snow. Ancient headstones leaned slightly toward each other like old friends sharing secrets of winters past. Rays of late-afternoon sunlight filtered lazily through the trees, painting the landscape with strokes of light and dark. Somewhere above, an owl hooted softly. Another day was drawing to a close.

_____

_____

_____

2. The abandoned graveyard lay empty and lifeless under the white scar of snow left by a storm the previous night. Long-forgotten gravestones tilted ominously in the dying sunlight. Naked trees, whose leaves had been stripped bare by icy blasts of wintry wind, now cast finger-like shadows across the frozen wasteland. The haunting call of an owl suddenly pierced the silence. Night was coming.

_____

_____

_____

B. What order did the writers of these passages follow when they arranged their details? How do you know?

_____

Descriptive Writing (continued)

C. Now prepare to write a description of your own.

1. In your journal brainstorm several places that you know well and that would make good subjects for a description. From this list, choose a favourite. In the blanks below, identify this place and try to identify the dominant impression you have of that place.

_____

_____

2. In your journal make a chart with the headings Sight, Hearing, Smell, Taste, and Touch. Under each heading, record as many details as you can that relate to that sense. If possible, go to this place with your journal and sit quietly for a while, and then record whatever impressions you have noted. Is your impression of this place the same as the one you recorded in Activity C1?

3. Look at the details you recorded on your chart and decide which ones best convey the dominant impression you are aiming for. Put check marks beside those you think are most useful.

4. Consider the best order for the details you have chosen. Will you present them in a spatial order (e.g., from near to far, from left to right), or in a time order (e.g., details that a person would notice first, second, third), or in some other order ?

_____

D. Write a draft of your description in your notebook or on a computer, making use of figurative language wherever possible. Choose specific nouns and vivid verbs that will generate strong impressions in your reader's mind.

E. When you have finished your first draft, put it aside for a day or two. Then read it again with the following questions in mind. Make any changes that will improve it.

1. Does my description begin and end smoothly?
2. Have I included details that appeal to as many senses as possible?
3. Have I made use of figurative language that generates strong impressions?
4. Have I used words whose connotations suit my purpose?
5. Have I arranged my details in a logical order that a reader can follow easily?
6. Does my description convey a single, main impression of the place?
7. Have I corrected all writing errors?

F. If possible, take a digital photograph of the place you have described, and post your photo and description on a class Web site.

UNIT
5

Exercise 28 (Grammar and Usage)

Compound Subjects and Predicates

Two or more simple subjects joined by the co-ordinating conjunctions *and, but,* or *or* form a **compound subject**.

EXAMPLE: **New Brunswick, Nova Scotia,** and **Prince Edward Island** *are called the Maritime provinces.*

Two or more verbs joined by the co-ordinating conjunctions *and, but,* or *or* form a **compound predicate**.

EXAMPLE: *The Saint John River* **flows** *through southern New Brunswick and* **empties** *into the Bay of Fundy.*

Often you can join two or more short sentences by using a compound subject or a compound predicate.

EXAMPLE: *The Haida live along the coast of British Columbia. The Nootka live in the same region.*
The Haida and Nootka live along the coast of British Columbia.

Change each of the following pairs of sentences into one well-written sentence with a compound subject or a compound predicate. Omit any unnecessary words.

1. Martin Frobisher searched for the Northwest Passage during the sixteenth century. John Davis looked at the same time.

   _____

   _____

   _____

2. Sir John Franklin sailed from England to look for the Passage in 1845. He had a crew of 105 men.

   _____

   _____

   _____

3. Thick timbers strengthened the hulls of Franklin's ships so they could withstand the tremendous pressure of the ice. They were also covered with iron plates.

   _____

   _____

   _____

4. When the ships became frozen in the ice, the crew decided to abandon the vessels. They tried to trudge across the frozen tundra to a fort further south.

   _____

   _____

   _____

REVIEW

A. Identify the type of writing technique (e.g., onomatopoeia, alliteration, simile, metaphor, personification) used in each sentence, and describe the effect intended by the writer.

1. The sloop slipped silently into the darkness.

   _____

2. Bells clanged as the bride and groom appeared on the church steps.

   _____

3. The dark clouds warned of an approaching storm.

   _____

4. The figure skater floated to a stop in front of the judges.

   _____

5. The man's whip-like voice made the child cry.

   _____

UNITS 1–5

B. Insert capital letters and commas where needed.

1. is judson planning to meet us at the airport on wednesday october 3?
2. my sister works at calhoon's carpets at 183 browning avenue winnipeg manitoba.
3. i took three pencils a calculator an eraser a compass and a protractor to write my math test.

C. Identify the three levels of language and give an example of when each might be used.

   _____

   _____

   _____

   _____

D. In the following sentences underline the nouns and circle the verbs. Above the nouns, tell whether they are proper, common, or compound. Above the verbs, tell whether they are transitive, intransitive, or linking.

1. Raoul waited on the steps of the library for three hours.

2. My sister always feels sick after she rides the roller coaster at Westwood Park.

Review (continued)

E. How can you tell the difference between a phrase and a clause?

_____

_____

F. Underline the complete subject in each sentence with one line and circle the simple subject. Underline the complete predicate in each sentence with two lines and circle the simple predicate.

1. The last marathon runner crossed the finish line a few minutes before midnight.

2. The fifteen weary travellers waited impatiently for the rain to stop.

G. Circle the co-ordinating conjunctions in the following sentences, and tell whether each sentence is simple or compound.

1. Kelcey and Darius left their bikes and backpacks at school. _____

2. You should phone or send us an e-mail when you arrive. _____

3. Everyone but Vanessa arrived early. _____

H. Read the following lead (beginning) of a hard news story and answer the questions that follow.

MILFORD—Two people were rushed to hospital yesterday when a propane barbecue ignited their tent at Grantwood Park.

1. Tell whether this lead does all the things a news lead should do. Support your ideas with examples.

_____

_____

_____

_____

2. What is the grammatical person used for the news story? How do you know?

_____

_____

3. Is this an appropriate person to use in the news story? Tell why or why not.

_____

_____

Exercise 29 (Study Skills)

Internet Research

The Internet has made it possible for writers to explore almost any topic. However, before using information they find on a Web site, writers must check to see whether it is reliable. One way of doing this is to see whether other sources present the same information. Another way is to examine the Web site carefully and ask the following questions:

1. What is the domain of the Web site? Educational (.edu) sites, government (.gov) sites, and organizational (.org) sites usually contain information that is more authoritative than information on personal Web sites.
2. Who created the site? Does this person or organization have special knowledge or experience that makes him, her, or it an authority on the topic?
3. Does the Web site present a detailed discussion of the topic or only a few brief points?
4. Does the Web site include a bibliography of sources? Are there links to other reliable sources?
5. Are all viewpoints about the topic presented, or does the Web site present the information from the point of view of only one person or organization?
6. Is the information factual or mostly opinion?
7. When was the information produced or updated? Is it current?

A. List below at least three topics that interest you. (You might want to refer to your journal and use some of the things you have been writing about.) Circle the one topic that interests you most right now.

_____

_____

_____

B. Do an Internet search for Web sites that contain information on the topic you circled above. Record below three sites you found; copy each address found in the location bar of your Web browser. Surround each address with angle brackets like these: < >

_____

_____

_____

C. Choose one of the Web sites you found and ask yourself the seven questions listed above. Write your responses in your notebook.

D. Use your responses to decide whether the Web site is reliable. In your notebook tell what you have decided and explain why.

_____

_____

Exercise 30 (Composition Construction)

Collecting Information

Before beginning to draft a piece, writers must take time to gather information. The first source that a writer can explore is personal knowledge. Writers often consider the following questions:

1.   What do I already know about this topic?
2.   What further information do I need?
3.   Where can I find this information?

Reference books, trade books, newspapers, magazines, and the Internet are a few sources of information, but they are not the only ones. Sometimes you may be able to talk to people who know a great deal about your subject. Before interviewing them, decide exactly what you want to ask. Keep an accurate record of their answers as well as the time, date, and place of the interview.

A. Suppose your teacher has asked you to write about the Loch Ness Monster. Imagine that all you know about the Loch Ness Monster is that it lives in a lake in Scotland. Before looking for further information, you decide there are four questions that you want answered. These are listed below, and the first three have been answered for you. Use at least two different sources to answer the fourth question.

1.   When was this monster first seen?

   Reports date back to the sixth century

   Road along north shore open in 1933

   Many sightings since then

2.   How many people have seen this monster?

   More than 1000 sightings

3.   How reliable are their reports?

   A number of photographs exist

   Many witnesses are trained observers

   such as soldiers, sailors, doctors

4.   What does the monster look like?

Collecting Information (continued)

B. Choose one of the following general topics:

1. my favourite sport
2. an unusual pet
3. an interesting hobby

Begin by narrowing your topic to one you could discuss in a paragraph six to ten sentences long.

In your notebook, list in point form what you already know about your topic.

Look over the information you listed. What further information do you need? On the following lines write five questions that you need answered. Use a variety of sources to find these answers. If possible, talk to people who are experts on your topic. Be sure to record each source of information.

Questions   **Answers**

1. _____   _____

   _____   _____

   _____   _____

2. _____   _____

   _____   _____

   _____   _____

3. _____   _____

   _____   _____

   _____   _____

4. _____   _____

   _____   _____

   _____   _____

5. _____   _____

   _____   _____

   _____   _____

UNIT
6

Exercise 31 (Study Skills)

Using Graphic Organizers

Often, writers have to make sense of a lot of information that they have found on a topic. One way to do this is to use graphic organizers. A graphic organizer is a visual way of organizing information or ideas. Writers use different kinds of organizers for different purposes.

In a **concept map**, a writer draws a bubble in the centre of a page and draws lines radiating from it to other bubbles. In the centre bubble the writer writes a topic and then fills in the other bubbles with ideas that relate to that topic. Writers often use concept maps to help them brainstorm what they already know about a topic. After researching a topic and making notes, writers often use graphic organizers like the concept map to help them make sense of what they have learned. This diagram shows a concept map that one student drew to brainstorm what he already knew about volcanoes.

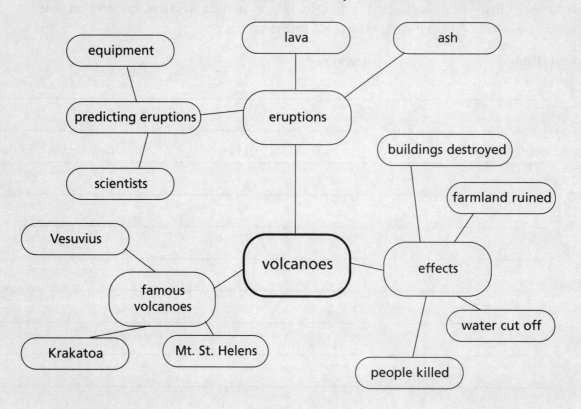

Another graphic organizer that is helpful for this purpose is an **inquiry chart**, which is a series of columns across a page. At the top of each column, writers jot down main ideas they have discovered about their topic, and then below that they record the details they have learned. They write briefly in point form and record the source of each piece of information. (Some writers use coloured highlighters for this purpose, choosing different colours to show information from different sources.) This diagram shows the main ideas the student used in his inquiry chart to group his information about volcanoes.

Causes of volcanic eruptions	Short-term effects of eruptions	Long-term effects of eruptions	Famous volcanoes

Using Graphic Organizers (continued)

A. Choose a topic that interests you. (You might want to refer to Activity A in Exercise 29 for suggestions.) Then, in the space below draw a concept map that illustrates what you already know about this topic.

UNIT
6

B. Find three sources of information that you could investigate to learn more about your topic. (You might want to refer to Activity B in Exercise 29 for sources.) Spend time examining these sources. Then, in your notebook or on chart paper, draw an inquiry chart that groups the information you have learned under three main headings. Write details in point form, but be sure to record the source of each piece of information. If you want, use different-coloured highlighters to indicate the different sources of information.

C. The concept map and inquiry chart are only two kinds of graphic organizers. Others include mindmaps, Venn diagrams, sequence charts, storyboards, pie charts, and many more, some of which you may already use in class or at home. Choose a graphic organizer that you are not familiar with and find out more about it, using dictionaries and the Internet. Prepare an example of the organizer and an explanation of its purpose.

Exercise 32 (Punctuation and Capitalization)

Parentheses and Dashes

Sometimes writers want to insert information within a sentence that will help make an idea clearer. Two forms of punctuation that are used for this purpose are parentheses and dashes.

Parentheses are always used in pairs. They enclose words, phrases, or sentences that add information directly related to what was previously stated. Writers also use parentheses to enclose letters or numbers that label items in a series.

EXAMPLE: *Shay priced items and set up displays (his usual duties) at the store.*
Our teacher asked us to identify the following information about the article: (1) the magazine it appeared in, (2) the date of its publication, (3) its author, and (4) the magazine's publisher.

Dashes may be used in pairs or individually. They are used in pairs when writers want to make a word or group of words stand out. When used individually, a dash indicates a sudden break or change in a sentence. A single dash can also indicate that a list will follow.

EXAMPLE: *The driver of the car—a man who had already been arrested twice for dangerous driving—was found responsible for the accident.*
Keegan waited for the pitch, saw the ball arc toward him, swung as hard as he could—and missed.
Two essential items are needed for any successful camping trip—a raincoat and a bottle of bug repellent.

Effective writers do not overuse parentheses or dashes. Too many of either can make writing seem choppy.

A. Copy the following sentences in your notebook. Place parentheses around information that has been inserted.

1. Taking two steps at a time as far as his short legs could reach, Jamie hurried toward the departure platform.

2. Ted's alarm did not go off he forgot to set it again, so he was late for class.

3. My cousin was able to move not lift but at least move two of the weights in the competition.

4. Cats creatures I could never stand are infuriatingly independent pets.

B. Copy the following sentences in your notebook. Insert dashes to make words stand out or to show a sudden break or change.

1. Julie made it clear that everything that happened whether good or bad was her responsibility.

2. Kyle asked everyone to bring an item for the food bank and everyone did except me.

3. The teacher sighed and asked Joe the only person who had done his homework to write his answer on the board.

4. Everybody who entered the classroom laughed at the poster until they realized who had drawn it.

Exercise 33 (Grammar and Usage)

Making Subjects and Verbs Agree

Subjects and verbs must agree in number. A singular subject takes a singular verb.
> EXAMPLE: The **train leaves** at 6:15 every morning.

A plural subject takes a plural verb.
> EXAMPLE: The four **trains leave** before 6:30 a.m.

To make a verb agree with its subject, ask yourself two questions: What is the subject? and, Is the subject singular or plural? Remember that most present tense verbs ending in -s or -es (runs, goes) are singular, but most nouns ending in -s or -es (cats, glasses, boxes) are plural.

A. Circle the form of the verb in parentheses that agrees with the subject.

> EXAMPLE: My mother (works, work) at the hospital.

1. My dentist (drills, drill).

2. The geese (waddles, waddle).

3. Our roof (leaks, leak).

4. The leaves (falls, fall).

5. All songs (ends, end).

6. Jordan (paints, paint).

7. Alligators (eats, eat).

8. Two students (wins, win).

9. Two men (walks, walk).

10. Her cat (sleeps, sleep).

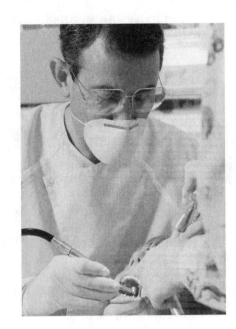

UNIT 6

B. In the blank write a subject that agrees in number with the boldface verb.

1. _____ **collects** old movies on DVD.

2. _____ **paint** portraits or seascapes.

3. _____ **walk** the dog every evening.

4. _____ **lives** three blocks from the school.

5. _____ **take** the shortcut through the park.

6. _____ **were broken** in the earthquake.

7. _____ always **starts** punctually.

Exercise 34 (Grammar and Usage)

Subject–Verb Agreement: Interrupting Words

When the simple subject is separated from the verb by a group of words (called a phrase), the verb must agree with the simple subject, rather than the noun in the phrase.

EXAMPLE: The **box** of apples **is** in the garage.

Sometimes people make mistakes when phrases beginning with *as well as, together with, like,* or *along with* come between the simple subject and the verb. Words in these phrases are not part of the simple subject.

EXAMPLE: The **coach**, along with six of his players, **was injured** in the accident.
  Four **nurses**, as well as a doctor, **were waiting** in the emergency ward.

A. In each sentence, circle the noun that is the simple subject. Write the form of the verb that agrees with the subject in the blank at the right.

1. The photographs in this book (was, were) taken by my father. _____

2. The glass in both bedroom windows (is, are) cracked. _____

3. The tin of cookies (is, are) on the kitchen table. _____

4. All the cows in that herd (is, are) Holsteins. _____

5. The brakes on the bicycle (is, are) not adjusted properly. _____

6. That large carton of towels (needs, need) to be repacked. _____

7. Every ticket for the play (has, have) been sold. _____

8. The captain, as well as the crew, (was, were) examined by the doctor. _____

9. The pears on the tree by the garage (is, are) much smaller than normal. _____

10. My younger sister, along with three of her friends, (has, have) gymnastic lessons today. _____

11. The musicians in that band (has, have) been selected from schools throughout the city. _____

12. A crate of oranges (costs, cost) seven dollars. _____

13. Both of the boys (likes, like) pepperoni pizza. _____

14. Everyone in science class (wants, want) be the one to make the winning project. _____

15. The teacher, unlike the students, (has, have) all the answers to the exam. _____

Exercise 35 (Composition Construction)

Putting Ideas in Order

Writing is **coherent** when ideas are arranged in a natural, sensible order that readers can understand easily. Ideas can be arranged in many ways. Details may be arranged in chronological order (e.g., from beginning to end), in order of importance (e.g., from least to most important), in place order (e.g., from left to right, from top to bottom, from near to far away), and so on.

A. Explain how each of the following sequences is organized.

1. sunbird, swallow, swan, tailorbird, tanager, thrush, turkey

   _____

2. breakfast, bus, bell, books

   _____

3. 1, 2, 4, 7, 11, 16, …

   _____

4. Quebec, Ontario, British Columbia, Alberta, Saskatchewan, Manitoba, Newfoundland and Labrador, New Brunswick, Nova Scotia, Prince Edward Island

   _____

5. coral, fish, wave, seagull, sky

   _____

6. red, orange, yellow, green, blue, violet

   _____

7. Victoria, Edmonton, Regina, Winnipeg, Toronto, Quebec City, Charlottetown, Fredericton, Halifax, St. John's

   _____

B. In your notebook rewrite each set of items in a logical order. Then explain why you organized the items this way. Use a different method to organize each set. Do not use alphabetical order.

1. Saturn, Jupiter, Mercury, Venus, Earth, Pluto, Uranus, Mars, Neptune
2. metre, kilometre, millimetre, decimetre, centimetre
3. Jean Chrétien, John Diefenbaker, Pierre Trudeau, Sir John A. Macdonald, W.L. Mackenzie King

Exercise 36 (Paragraph Construction)

Writing the Topic Sentence

A well-written **topic sentence** identifies the main idea of a paragraph and catches the reader's attention. All the other sentences must relate to or explain that one idea. One of the easiest ways to organize a paragraph is to begin with a topic sentence. Then write a series of detailed sentences that develop or support the main idea. Note how the first sentence of the following paragraph summarizes what will follow.

To survive, desert plants must be able to react quickly to rare cloudbursts. The seeds of many plants lie dormant in the barren soil until they are soaked by brief spring rains. The new plants grow rapidly, and soon their flowers dot the desert with bright patches of colour. For a few glorious weeks the desert is alive with bloom. The intense heat of the sun, however, promptly puts an end to this bright show. Flowers, leaves, and stems wither and disappear. But nature's purpose has been served. Billions of seeds have dropped to the ground to await the next rainfall.

A. Look back at the work you did for Activity B in Exercise 30.

1. Read the information you collected for that activity and choose your main idea. Then write a topic sentence for your paragraph. Make sure your sentence is interesting and lets your reader know right away what your paragraph will be about.

   _____

   _____

2. Write the first draft of your paragraph.

   _____

   _____

   _____

   _____

   _____

3. Ask yourself the following questions:

   a. Does my topic sentence identify the main idea of my paragraph in an interesting way?

   b. Does everything in my paragraph relate to my topic sentence?

B. Imagine you could meet any character from history. Whom would you choose?

1. Write your choice in your notebook.

2. Now you need to learn as much as you can about the person you have chosen. In your notebook write five questions you would like answered about this person.

3. Use a variety of sources to find the answers to your questions. Write your answers in point form and record the source(s) of your information.

4. Using the information you have collected, repeat Activity A above.

Exercise 37 (Paragraph Construction)

Placing the Topic Sentence

The topic sentence does not have to appear at the beginning of a paragraph. Writers vary the placement of their topic sentences to make their paragraphs more interesting to read. For example, writers sometimes choose to catch their readers' attention with one or two interesting comments before stating their topic sentence.

> EXAMPLE: *Participating in team sports is an excellent way to build strong bodies, develop teamwork skills, and have fun at the same time. Playing on teams can be especially beneficial for young people who are just learning how to cooperate and work with their peers.* **However, some parents unwittingly make their children's involvement in team sports a negative experience.** *For example, a few parents may have unrealistic expectations of their children's athletic abilities. This can lead to frustration and anxiety for some children who may feel they can never be "good enough." As well, a few parents mistakenly believe that success in sports is measured only in wins, conveying the impression that losing a competition means only failure when, in fact, children can and should take pride in playing fairly and playing well.*

At other times, a writer may place the topic sentence at the end of a paragraph to sum up the ideas.

> EXAMPLE: *According to my brother, dogs are easily trained but cats are far more independent and seldom can be relied on to perform even the simplest tasks. Dogs, he says, often alert their owners to trespassers and burglars, whereas cats tend to disappear when strangers arrive on the scene. Moreover, he says that dogs are more openly affectionate to and appreciative of their owners than are cats.* **It is clear that my brother believes dogs are far superior to cats in many ways.**

Return to the paragraphs you wrote in Exercise 36 and rewrite them using the two topic sentence arrangements demonstrated above. Do you prefer the new versions more or less than your original arrangement? Why?

_____

_____

_____

_____

_____

_____

_____

_____

_____

_____

Subject–Verb Agreement: Making Verbs Agree with Compound Subjects

You have learned that a **compound subject** is two or more subjects that share the same verb. Often, the parts of a compound subject are joined by the words *and* or *or*. Sometimes *either/or* or *neither/nor* are used to link simple subjects. When the parts of the compound subject are joined by *and*, use a plural verb.

> EXAMPLE: **Mount McKinley** and **Mount Logan** are the highest mountains in North America.

When the parts of the compound subject are joined by *or, either/or,* or *neither/nor,* the verb agrees with the subject closer to the verb.

> EXAMPLE: Neither **Mercury** nor **Mars** is as large as Earth.
> Neither the **girls** nor their **teacher** has much canoeing experience.
> Neither the **teacher** nor the **girls** have much canoeing experience.

A. Circle the compound subjects in the following sentences. Choose the correct form of the verb from the two in parentheses and write it in the blank at the right.

> EXAMPLE: Either the principal or the secretary always
> (unlocks, unlock) the door at eight o'clock.   *unlocks*

1. Oboes, clarinets, and flutes (forms, form) the woodwind section of the orchestra.

   _____

2. Neither my mother nor my father (likes, like) watching soap operas.

   _____

3. Neither Ovid nor his brothers (has, have) taken a course in wilderness survival.

   _____

4. The computer's disk drives or its monitor (needs, need) adjustment.

   _____

5. Either rags or pulpwood (is, are) used in making paper.

   _____

6. Neither the suspended players nor their coach (was, were) allowed to speak to the reporters.

   _____

7. Neither the blankets nor the drapes (was, were) delivered to the right house.

   _____

8. Alexandra and Adam (is, are) harvesting their potato crop this week.

   _____

9. A pointer or a setter (makes, make) an excellent hunting dog.

   _____

10. Hawks and owls (has, have) sharp, curved claws to help catch their prey.

   _____

Subject–Verb Agreement: Making Verbs Agree with Compound Subjects (continued)

B. Circle the compound subjects in each of the following sentences. Choose the correct form of the verb from the two in parentheses and write it in the blank at the right. Below each, give a reason for your choice.

1. Either the duck hawk or the golden eagle (is, are) the fastest flying bird. _____

   _____

2. Nathan and Indra (belongs, belong) to the chess club. _____

   _____

3. Dacron or goose down (makes, make) excellent filler material for sleeping bags. _____

   _____

4. Neither the apron nor the shirts (has, have) been ironed. _____

   _____

5. Either Mr. Chiu or his brother (knows, know) the combination for that lock. _____

   _____

6. Almost every summer, high winds or hail (damages, damage) the crops in this region. _____

   _____

7. Either Saskia or Fiona (is, are) responsible for collecting the money. _____

   _____

8. Every time Liam or Jared (wash, washes) the dishes, something gets broken. _____

   _____

9. Julia and her family (lives, live) in Iqaluit. _____

   _____

10. Alligators, crocodiles, snakes, and turtles (is, are) reptiles. _____

   _____

UNIT
7

Exercise 39 (Grammar and Usage)

Subject–Verb Agreement: When Subjects Follow the Verb

In most English sentences, the subject comes before the verb. However, if a sentence begins with the introductory words *here* or *there*, the subject usually follows the verb. When you start a sentence with one of these words, ask yourself this question: Will the subject be singular or plural? Use the verb form that agrees with the subject.

EXAMPLE: Here **is** the **answer** to your question. (singular verb, singular subject)
There **are** three **locks** on the back door. (plural verb, plural subject)

The verb is also likely to come before the subject in sentences that ask questions.
EXAMPLE: Where **are** the **keys** for the equipment room? (plural verb, plural subject)

A. Under the words **Subject** and **Verb**, write the simple subject and verb for each sentence.

	Subject	Verb
1. How much do those hamburgers cost?	_____	_____
2. Has your sister visited Sir John A. Macdonald's home in Kingston?	_____	_____
3. There are two ways to solve the problem.	_____	_____
4. Is your mother or father at home?	_____	_____
5. Here comes the bus!	_____	_____
6. Do your brothers have tickets to the game?	_____	_____
7. Here are some new spokes for your bicycle.	_____	_____
8. There are still three test tubes missing.	_____	_____
9. Where are the students who volunteered?	_____	_____
10. Are there any oranges left?	_____	_____
11. There goes the coach.	_____	_____
12. Is your backpack the purple one?	_____	_____
13. There are three pieces of pecan pie in the fridge.	_____	_____
14. Is there a snack for me?	_____	_____
15. Here is your skateboard.	_____	_____

Subject–Verb Agreement: When Subjects Follow the Verb (continued)

B. Circle the simple subject in each sentence. Above each subject write *P* if it is plural, and *S* if it is singular. In the blank following each sentence, write the correct form of the verb.

1. Here (comes, come) the marching band from Seaview School. _____

2. (Does, Do) those library books have to be returned? _____

3. (Has, Have) those horses been fed? _____

4. There (was, were) a box of potatoes in the garage. _____

5. When (was, were) your brothers going to Japan? _____

6. Here (is, are) the plans for the birdhouse. _____

7. (There's, There are) times when I wish I were an adult. _____

8. (Are, Is) there too many people in that boat? _____

9. In the den (was, were) four coyote pups. _____

10. (There's, There are) ten girls on the track team. _____

11. (Where's, Where are) the tickets to the football game? _____

12. There (was, were) only three fish in the tank. _____

13. (Has, Have) the broken stairs been repaired? _____

14. Counting today, (there's, there are) only ten days left. _____

15. (Wasn't, Weren't) the French army defeated at Waterloo? _____

UNIT 7

C. When you edit your work, be sure to check for subject–verb agreement. The following paragraphs have eight verbs that do not agree with their subjects. Circle each faulty verb and write the correct form in the margin.

The National Park at Point Pelee on Lake Ontario is a special place for many reasons. Since it's located on both the Atlantic and the Mississippi flyways, migrating birds, bats, and insects is funnelled through the park. From the air, the point is a recognizable landmark that invites birds to land. To date, more than 330 species of birds has been sighted in the park, and bird watchers sometimes spots as many as 150 different species in a day.

There's many forms of plant and animal life found in the park. Although it contain only sixteen square kilometres, Pelee has more than 750 species of plants. Some of these plants, such as the prickly pear cactus, is now rare in Canada. The waters of Lake Erie tempers the park's climate and gives the area one of the longest frost-free growing seasons in Canada.

Exercise 40 (Grammar and Usage)

Subject–Verb Agreement: Some Special Problems

Take care when you use a noun ending in -s as the simple subject of a sentence. Many of these words, such as *physics, mumps, dominoes,* and *United States,* have a plural form but a singular meaning.

> EXAMPLE: **Mathematics** *is a required course in grade eight.*
> **Measles** *causes a red rash to appear on the skin.*
> **The United Nations** *was set up in 1945.*

Most nouns ending in -s, however, are plural. Words such as *scissors, trousers, pants, tongs, tweezers, wages,* and *pliers* are plural in meaning and require a plural verb.

> EXAMPLE: *Those* **scissors** *are exceptionally sharp.*
> *My* **wages** *have not increased.*

Collective nouns are another group that can cause problems. These nouns can take either a singular or a plural verb depending on how they are used. Use a singular verb when the group acts as a unit.

> EXAMPLE: *Our hockey* **team** *has won its last five games.*

Use a plural verb when the group acts as a collection of individuals.

> EXAMPLE: *The winning* **team** *have received their trophies.*

Circle the simple subject in each sentence. In the blank write the form of the verb in parentheses that agrees with this subject.

1. The latest news from the hijacked plane (is, are) encouraging. _____

2. The city council (meets, meet) Tuesday night. _____

3. The Philippines (has, have) a warm, humid climate. _____

4. Those trousers (needs, need) ironing. _____

5. Mumps (causes, cause) glands in the neck to swell. _____

6. Checkers (requires, require) both skill and concentration. _____

7. The tongs (is, are) hanging beside the fireplace. _____

8. Our family (is, are) unable to agree on where to go for a holiday this summer. _____

9. Our family (is, are) going to the football game on Saturday. _____

10. The Netherlands (export, exports) large quantities of cheese. _____

11. The orchestra (is, are) playing a symphony by Beethoven. _____

12. The team from Macdonald School (is, are) in first place. _____

Exercise 41 (Grammar and Usage)

Helping Verbs

Sometimes a verb form is made up of more than one word. The key word, which names the action, is called the **main verb**, or **principal verb**. The verb parts that come before the main verb are called **helping verbs**, or **auxiliary verbs**. The main verb, when joined with any helping verbs, creates a **verb phrase**.

EXAMPLE: Shayla **has won** the trophy six times.

Some sentences have two or three helping verbs before the main verb.

EXAMPLE: The broken window **should have been fixed** yesterday.

Sometimes the main verb is separated from its helpers by one or more words that are not verbs. *Not* and the contraction *n't*, for example, often interrupt verb phrases.

EXAMPLE: Those doors **should** not **be locked** before six o'clock.
Celine **will** probably not **play** goal on Saturday.

The following verbs are often used as helping verbs:

am	was	be	has	do	must	can	will	shall
is	were	been	have	does	may	could	would	should
are		had	did	might				

The following sentences contain one main verb in each sentence and fourteen helping verbs altogether. Draw a circle around each main verb, and underline the helping verbs. Remember that a verb phrase may be interrupted by one or more words.

1. Our neighbour was seriously injured in a traffic accident last year.

2. My sister is studying medicine at Dalhousie University in Halifax.

3. The Dionne quintuplets were born at Corbell, Ontario, on May 24, 1934.

4. The Trans-Canada Highway through Kicking Horse Pass will probably not be open until Tuesday.

5. Each of the students has just completed a project on the St. Lawrence Seaway.

6. My grandparents have just moved to Thunder Bay.

7. The students from Yellowknife should have arrived on the eleven o'clock flight.

8. In July, Dr. Leung will be studying the vegetation near Wapta Lake in Yoho National Park.

9. The province of Alberta has been producing most of Canada's oil since 1941.

10. Many of the farmers south of Regina are harvesting their grain this week.

UNIT
8

Exercise 42 (Grammar and Usage)

Verb Tenses

One way of showing time in English is to use words and expressions such as *yesterday, after supper,* and *before long.* Another way is through the tense of the verb in the sentence. The **present tense** expresses action that is happening now.
  EXAMPLE: *My brothers* **play** *hockey for the Brandon Wheat Kings.*

The **past tense** expresses action that took place in the past. To form the past tense of most regular verbs, add *-ed.*
  EXAMPLE: *My brothers* **played** *hockey for the Brandon Wheat Kings.*

The **future tense** expresses action that will take place in the future. This tense is formed by adding the helping verbs *shall* or *will* to the present form.
  EXAMPLE: *My brothers* **will play** *hockey for the Brandon Wheat Kings.*

You can use either the past or the present tense to describe past events. If you want your description to sound serious and matter-of-fact, use the past tense. If you want your reader to feel as if he or she is really there, choose the present tense.

A. Circle each verb and identify its tense.

1. Ian lifts weights every Thursday at the fitness centre. _____

2. The principal will hold an assembly during last period. _____

3. Jacob found some money in the locker room. _____

4. Carly ate two hot dogs and some popcorn at the carnival this morning. _____

5. You'll like this video. _____

6. Collette and Marianne take tennis lessons together. _____

7. Jamal will enter the skateboard competition. _____

B. Imagine you are a newspaper writer. Think of someone real or imaginary who would have been at one of the following historical events. Then imagine interviewing this person. In your notebook write two versions of his or her account of the events. Use the past tense in the first story; use the present tense in the second.

1. A member of John Cabot's crew who arrived on the east coast of Canada in 1497.

2. A worker on the Canadian Pacific Railway who has just been rescued from a Rogers Pass avalanche.

3. A prospector in Yukon in 1898 who discovered a rich vein of gold.

4. A Canadian soldier who landed on the coast of France during the Second World War.

5. A Canadian athlete at the Olympic Games who won a gold medal.

Exercise 43 (Word Skills)

Choosing Vivid Verbs

Like specific nouns, vivid verbs generate strong impressions in the minds of readers. Colourless verbs identify actions that can be performed in a variety of ways; vivid verbs identify actions that can be performed in only one way.

> *EXAMPLE:* *run* (a colourless verb)
> *scamper, scurry, jog, dash, sprint, trot, gallop, bolt* (vivid verbs)

Whenever possible, replace colourless verbs with vivid verbs in your writing.

A. *Walk* is a colourless verb because this action can be performed in many different ways. In your notebook explain the impression created by each of the following vivid verbs:

1. shuffled
2. strolled
3. marched
4. staggered
5. plodded
6. stalked
7. strutted
8. paced

B. On the line below each sentence, write at least three vivid verbs to replace the colourless verb in boldface type. Circle the verb you feel is most effective in each group. Write interesting sentences in your notebook using the verbs you circled.

1. "Don't ever do that again!" **said** Karima.

   _____

2. The small child opened the door a crack and **looked** out.

   _____

3. When my younger brother cleans up his room, he **puts** all his belongings in the closet.

   _____

4. The deadly rattlesnake **came** slowly toward my hiding place.

   _____

5. The terrified ground squirrel **ran** for its burrow when the hawk appeared.

   _____

6. "Please don't leave me alone with that dog!" **said** the terrified prisoner.

   _____

UNIT
8

Exercise 44 (Paragraph Construction)

Transitional Expressions

Writers use words or phrases called **transitional expressions** to help readers follow the order of a piece of writing. The following are only a few of these transitional expressions:
- first, second, third, finally (time)
- less significant, more important (importance)
- on the top, in the middle, at the bottom (place)
- one difference, on the one hand, on the other hand (contrast)
- in addition, furthermore (similarity)
- as a result (cause and effect)
- in conclusion (summary)

A. The following passage, describing the sinking of the luxury liner *Titanic*, is in chronological (time) order. Read the passage carefully and underline all the transitional expressions the writer has used to show how the events are related in time.

The *Titanic*'s problems began at 11:45 p.m. on April 14, 1912, when the massive ship slammed into a North Atlantic iceberg, ripping a huge ninety-metre gash down the right side of the hull. Almost immediately seawater flooded into five of the sixteen watertight compartments. Thirty-five minutes after the collision, the *Titanic*'s radio operator sent out "CQD" (come quickly disaster). At 12:45 a.m. the crew lowered the first of the liner's twenty lifeboats. During the next ninety minutes, many lifeboats pulled away only partly full, as passengers simply couldn't believe the *Titanic* actually was sinking. Finally, just two hours and forty minutes after striking the iceberg, the *Titanic* plunged to the bottom with more than 1500 of the 2224 passengers and crew.

B. Choose one of the following topic sentences. In your notebook, list five events that could make up a story. Arrange these events in chronological order, and then use them to write a narrative paragraph. Be sure to add transitional expressions to tie the events together.

1. Suddenly the accelerator jammed, and the car careened out of control down the steep hill toward the river.
2. Slowly a panel on the side of the ship slid open, and two creatures from another world tumbled onto our lawn.
3. With tears streaming down her face, my sister met me at the front door with the shocking news.
4. Yes, he was after me again, and this time I knew I was really in trouble!
5. I huddled motionless as the strange brute wriggled slowly toward my hiding place at the end of the abandoned tunnel.

Exercise 45 (Grammar and Usage)

Active and Passive Voice

The **voice** of a verb shows the relationship between the subject of the sentence and the action expressed by the verb. When the subject is performing the action, the verb is said to be in the **active voice**.

*EXAMPLE: Katrina **stacked** the boxes on the deck.*

When the subject of the verb is the receiver of the action, the verb is said to be in the **passive voice**.

*EXAMPLE: The boxes **were stacked** by Katrina.*

In this sentence the simple subject *boxes* is the receiver of the verb *were stacked*.

Verbs in the passive voice are made up of a form of the verb *to be* along with a past participle. The forms of *to be* used for the passive voice are *is, are, was, were, has been, have been,* and *had been*.

Use the active voice as much as possible in your own writing. Verbs in the passive voice can sound weak and wordy.

Circle the passive verbs in these sentences. On the line below each sentence, rewrite the sentence by changing the verb to the active voice. In most of the sentences you will have to provide your own subject.

EXAMPLE: The security system was turned on about ten o'clock.

The guard turned on the security system about ten o'clock.

1. The leak in the gas pipe has been repaired.

   _____

2. The rabbits in those pens are fed twice a day.

   _____

3. The skiers were found huddled under a large spruce tree.

   _____

4. All the valuable paintings were destroyed in the fire.

   _____

5. The ball was hit over the right-field fence.

   _____

6. At the end of the ceremony the flag was slowly lowered.

   _____

UNIT
9

7. The awards were presented in the gymnasium.

   _____

8. My guitar was given to me by my aunt.

   _____

Writing a Business Letter

Letters to companies, organizations, or businesspeople are called business letters. They usually follow one of three forms: block, modified block, or semiblock. The sample letter on the opposite page follows the block form. All business letters have six main parts. In the sample letter, note how these parts are arranged on the page.

A. The **heading** is the complete mailing address of the sender, followed by the date.

B. The **inside address** includes the receiver's name, address, and title (if known).

C. The **salutation** is the greeting. If possible, include the receiver's name (e.g., Ms. Tomlinson, Mr. Chen) in the salutation. If the receiver's name is not known, the sender may write *To Whom It May Concern* or *Dear Sir or Madam.* The salutation in a business letter is usually followed by a colon.

D. The **body** of a business letter should be clear, concise, correct, complete, and courteous.

E. The **closing** politely concludes the letter and is always followed by a comma. Only the first letter of the closing is capitalized.

F. The sender's name appears twice at the end of the letter: as a **signature** below the closing, then typed or printed below the signature.

Here are some guidelines to follow in writing a business letter.

- Be sure your letter does not contain writing errors, such as spelling or grammatical mistakes. It is wise to write a first draft and edit it carefully before writing the final copy you will send.
- If possible, type your letter or produce it on a computer. If this is not possible, write it neatly in ink. Always use plain paper, preferably 21 cm by 28 cm in size.
- Make sure the margins on the left and right are equal and at least 2.5 cm wide. The top and bottom margins should be equal.
- Write on one side of the paper only.
- Be brief and to the point. Businesspeople are busy.
- If you type or word process your letter, you may double space between paragraphs as an alternative to indenting the paragraphs.

Block	Modified Block	Semiblock
Dear _____ : Yours truly,	Dear _____ : Yours truly,	Dear _____ : Yours truly,

Writing a Business Letter (continued)

A
88 Water St.
Campbellton, NB E3N 3G7
March 28, 2004

B
The Manager
Travel Manitoba
Legislative Building
Winnipeg, MB R3C 0V8

C Dear Madam or Sir:

D My family will be vacationing in Manitoba in July, and we require information that will help us plan our time there. We are particularly interested in cycling, wilderness canoeing, and sailing. Please send us material on cycling trails in the provincial parks. We would also like some information on the Boissevain Turtle Derby and the St. Pierre-Jolys Frog Follies.

As we will be travelling in an RV, we would also appreciate receiving a list of campgrounds in Manitoba.

Thank you very much for your help.

E Sincerely yours,

F *Denise Nadeau*

Denise Nadeau

Use your imagination. Imagine it is now the year 2075 and space flights to the planet Mars leave from Vancouver and Toronto every Saturday. On a computer or in your notebook write a letter to the manager of the Mars tourist office, inquiring about vacation possibilities on the planet.

**UNIT
9**

Uses of the Colon and Semicolon

A **colon** appears after the salutation in a business letter, but it is also used to introduce a list of items. An independent (main) clause must always come before a colon when it introduces a list.

> EXAMPLE: *Juan found the following things on the bus: two backpacks, a brush, a ring, three magazines, and a purse.*

A colon is also used between two main (independent) clauses when the second clause explains the first. The first word of the second clause is not capitalized unless it is a proper noun.

> EXAMPLE: *Plants use a process called photosynthesis: they manufacture carbohydrates from carbon dioxide and water, using light as an energy source.*

A **semicolon** joins two main (independent) clauses that are closely related *without* using a co-ordinating conjunction.

> EXAMPLE: *We arrived at the movies late; we missed the film's opening credits.*

A semicolon is also used to separate items in a series if one or more of these items contain commas.

> EXAMPLE: *James was so determined to save enough money for university that he worked at two part-time jobs during the school year; ran errands, painted houses, and walked dogs for neighbours; and invested all his earnings in a savings bond.*

Add colons and semicolons where necessary to the following sentences. Not all of the sentences require punctuation to be added.

1. Jordan was certain of one thing he had not passed the exam.

2. Lauren chose tulips, daffodils, and petunias for the flowerbed in the back yard.

3. For the trip, Brandon bought crackers, chips, and chocolate bars, pop, juice, and mineral water, and peanuts, cashews, and hazelnuts.

4. Be sure to pack the following items in a carry-on bag T-shirts, shorts, insect repellent, and sunblock.

5. Daniel had already sent his application, but Suzanne had not completed hers.

6. We knew why our teacher had told us to put away our books he was giving another surprise quiz.

7. I am available to work after school on Mondays, Wednesdays, and Fridays, on Saturday mornings, and on Tuesday, Thursday, and Friday evenings.

8. The horse snorted and reared Collette yelled for us to get back.

Exercise 48 (Word Skills)

Canadian Spelling

Not all English-speaking countries spell English words the same way. Canadian spelling is, in fact, a mixture of British and American spellings. For example, the Canadian spelling of *catalogue* is the same as the British spelling but different from the American *catalog*. But the Canadian spelling of *analyze* is the same as the American spelling but different from the British *analyse*. In the past many Canadians used both American and British spellings; however, recently, more people have become interested in identifying accepted Canadian spellings, and the Canadian Press news agency now encourages the use of Canadian spellings in the media. Correct Canadian spelling is generally accepted to be the spelling of words used in the *Hansard*, the official transcript of the proceedings of the Parliament of Canada, which represents all Canadians.

A. Below are the British, American, and Canadian spellings of some common words. In your notebook summarize the feature of Canadian spelling that is illustrated by each group. Then add two Canadian spellings to each group.

1.

British	**American**	**Canadian**
colour	color	colour
labour	labor	labour
rumour	rumor	rumour

2.

British	**American**	**Canadian**
civilisation	civilization	civilization
criticise	criticize	criticize
realise	realize	realize

3.

British	**American**	**Canadian**	
fibre	fiber	fibre	
metre	meter	metre	(unit of length)
meter	meter	meter	(measuring device, e.g., gas meter)
theatre	theater	theatre	

B. Using a Canadian dictionary or an online source of Canadian spellings, find the Canadian spelling of the following words. You have been given the first letter of each word.

1. you cash this at a bank   *c* _____

2. the permit that allows someone to drive a car   *l* _____

3. the vehicle that clears roads in winter   *p* _____

4. a violation of a criminal code   *o* _____

5. the person who lives next door to you   *n* _____

6. to guide a vehicle around obstacles   *m* _____

7. a person who offers guidance in personal or career matters   *c* _____

UNIT
10

Exercise 49 (Study Skills)

Brushing Up on Dictionary Skills

The dictionary is one of the most valuable reference books a writer can use. The words listed alphabetically in boldface type in a dictionary are called **entry words**, and a single dictionary entry, like the one below, can include many pieces of information.

A   B   C D

har·ness (hŏr′nĭs) *n.* **1.** The gear or tackle, other than a yoke, with which a draft

E   animal pulls a vehicle or an implement. **2.** Something resembling such gear or tackle, as the straps used to hold a parachute to the body. **3.** A device that raises and lowers the warp threads on a loom. **4.** *Archaic.* Armour for a man or horse. – *tr.v.* **-nessed, -ness·ing, -ness·es. 1.a.** To put a harness on (a draft animal). **b.** To fasten by the use of a harness. **2.** To bring under control and direct the force of. – *idiom.* **in harness.** On duty or at work. [ME *harnes* <OFr. *harneis,* of Gmc. orig. See nes-1*.]

F   G   H

The entry word (A) gives the correct spelling of the word and is capitalized only if the word is a proper noun. The dot between the "r" and the "n" shows you where to break the word into syllables.

Right after the entry word is a respelling of the word (B), showing how it is pronounced. The accent mark (C) indicates that the first syllable is stressed in this word. The italic letters (D) indicate which part of speech the following meanings apply to, in this example *n.* for noun and *tr.v.* for transitive verb.

The word *Archaic* (E) indicates a meaning that is now uncommon. The "a." and "b." division in the first meaning for the verb (F) indicates closely related meanings. The phrase "in harness" is labelled *idiom* (G), which means it cannot be understood from the individual words in the phrase. The etymology (the history of the word's origin) (H) appears in the square brackets at the end of the definition.

Often dictionaries list several different and unrelated meanings for the same word. A *bridge*, for example, can be "something built over a river or road so that people, cars, or trains can get across," "the platform above the deck of a ship for the officer in command," or "the upper, bony part of the nose." Within the dictionary entry, each new meaning is introduced with a letter or a number. Most dictionaries list the most common definitions of the word first.

A. Try answering the following questions by circling one of the choices. Then check a dictionary to see how many you answered correctly.

1. If you were a *pyromaniac*, would you enjoy (a) eating pies, (b) starting fires, or (c) watching fireworks?

2. If you had broken your *ulna*, would a doctor put a cast on (a) your leg, (b) your arm, or (c) your foot?

3. Would you pronounce *indict* to rhyme with (a) hermit, (b) polite, or (c) restrict?

4. Would a *lepidopteran* have (a) wings, (b) hooves, or (c) a long tail?

5. If a piece of music is marked *fortissimo*, should it be played (a) as quickly as possible, (b) as softly as possible, or (c) as loudly as possible?

6. Is a *soupçon* (a) a private conversation, (b) a very small amount, or (c) a container for soup?

7. Is a *neophyte* (a) a rare mineral, (b) a beginner, or (c) a sea god in Greek mythology?

Brushing Up on Dictionary Skills (continued)

B. Some of the following words need capital letters. Use your dictionary to find out which letters should be capitalized. Then circle them.

german shepherd   morse code   spanish rice   grey cup

south pole   juneberry   southpaw   olympic games

C. The following words are often pronounced incorrectly. Look up the pronunciation of each word in your dictionary. In the blank after each word, write a rhyming word.

EXAMPLE: ballet _today_

1. heir _____

2. lyre _____

3. corps _____

4. aisle _____

5. debris _____

6. yacht _____

7. quay _____

8. brooch _____

9. feign _____

10. dough _____

D. Find each word in boldface type below in your dictionary. Read all the definitions for each entry. On the line below each sentence, write the meaning that fits best.

1. Shannon hopes to be **cast** as the villain in the school play.

   _____

2. The sailors couldn't **right** the overturned boat.

   _____

3. He usually spends Friday evening in the officers' **mess**.

   _____

4. The ranchers drove the wild horses into a **blind** canyon.

   _____

5. When the prime minister entered the room, the guards **snapped** to attention.

   _____

6. Pioneers in Canada often **cured** their meat by drying and salting it.

   _____

7. My mother won the turkey in a **draw** at her office.

   _____

UNIT
10

Uses of the Hyphen

An important use of the hyphen is to break a long word at the end of a line so it may be continued on the following line. The word must always be broken between syllables. However, if a syllable with only one or two letters appears on a line, it is better to write the entire word on one line. One-syllable words cannot be hyphenated.

EXAMPLE: *The harbour authorities had not yet determined the nationality of the stowaway.*

Hyphens are used in fractions and in compound numbers from twenty-one to ninety-nine.

EXAMPLE: *one-half   five-sixths   forty-two   seventy-six*

Some compound nouns contain hyphens.

EXAMPLE: *self-respect   mother-in-law*

Hyphens are used between words that make up a compound adjective when the compound adjective is written *before* the noun. A hyphen is not used when the compound adjective *follows* the noun.

EXAMPLE: *Saskia turned in a well-written essay.
Saskia's essay was well written.*

A hyphen is not used between an adverb ending in *-ly* and an adjective preceding the noun.

EXAMPLE: *It was an awkwardly drawn illustration.*

A. In these words draw a vertical line between syllables where a hyphen could properly break the word at the end of a line. (Remember, a syllable that is only one or two letters long should not appear on a line by itself.) Then use a dictionary to check your work.

1. postoperative
2. diorama
3. favourable
4. kinesiology
5. residual
6. unceremoniously
7. thermonuclear
8. musculoskeletal
9. geranium

B. Add hyphens where necessary to the following sentences. Not all of the sentences require hyphens. For those sentences that do not require hyphens, be prepared to explain why.

1. Two best selling authors will give readings at the Gander Public Library tonight.

2. Susan Hinton was sixteen years old when she wrote her first novel, *The Outsiders.*

3. I found an advertisement for a cheap, slightly used sofa.

4. Two thirds of the pie had been eaten before we got home.

5. My aunt retired when she was fifty three years old.

6. Most parents recognize the importance of self esteem in their children.

7. Her father in law was late for the reception.

8. The person who spoke to our class was a well known cancer survivor.

Exercise 51 (Word Skills)

Using Spell-Checker Software

Most word-processing programs include spell-checker applications that alert writers to spelling errors. Some applications operate continually in the background, automatically highlighting words that are keyed incorrectly, while others can be run as a separate process. When using either application, remember three important weaknesses of spell-checker software:

1. American-made programs often highlight Canadian spellings as incorrect, even when such programs allow the user to select the nationality of the language being used.
   EXAMPLE: The soccer player seemed to favour his right leg when he got up.

2. Many spell-checker programs will not alert the user to usage errors; that is, when a word is used incorrectly, but it is a real word that the spell checker does not identify as wrong. For example, most spell-checker software will not recognize that the word *it's* is used incorrectly in the following sentence:
   EXAMPLE: The dog tugged at it's leash.

3. Spell-checker applications can be annoying when writers intentionally use slang or phonetically spelled words where their use is acceptable, such as in dialogue. Such software can be especially frustrating if it automatically corrects common errors.
   EXAMPLE: "Yo, whazzup?" the skater said as he high-fived his buddy.

Although spell-checker applications are very helpful tools for writers, they do not lessen the need for sound knowledge of spelling and word use. Be sure to consider carefully every word a spell checker highlights, and remember that most spell checkers will not recognize usage problems.

A. The following passage has had a spell check run on it using a software program. The words that the program identified as incorrect have been highlighted. Read the passage carefully to see whether the program has correctly identified all changes that need to be made in the passage. Put a check mark beside each word the spell checker correctly questioned. Put an X beside each highlighted word that you would deliberately keep as it appears. Underline any incorrect words the program missed.

"Do you no whether Scott is still meetin' us here?" Megan asked Pete. She ran a hand impateintly through her long curley hare and sighed. She had been waiting outside the CD store for nearly half an hour. "I'm not gonna sit here much longer."

Pete shruged his shoulders and glanced at his watch again. "I dunno. I was sure Scott said he'd be hear by now." He scanned the crowd of shoppers streaming threw the entrance. "Hey! Their he is now!"

B. If you use a word-processing program with a spell-checker application, explore the program's Menu or Help windows to learn about its various spell-checker features. In your notebook identify the program and list four or five spell-checker features you have identified.

Exercise 52 (Sentence Construction)

Subordinating Conjunctions and Complex Sentences

In Exercise 21 you learned that an independent (or main) clause makes a complete thought and can stand alone as a sentence. A dependent (or subordinate) clause cannot stand alone as a sentence.

A dependent clause begins with a joining word called a **subordinating conjunction**. The following are only a few examples of subordinating conjunctions:

after	as far as	because	if	so that	until
although	as if	before	rather than	when	whenever
as	as long as	even though	since	unless	while

Note that dependent clauses need something else to complete their meaning.

EXAMPLE: **When** the guards turned their backs
Once the maintenance crew had cleared the runway

The reader wants to know what happened "When the guards turned their backs" and "Once the maintenance crew had cleared the runway." We can complete the meaning of each dependent clause by adding an independent clause.

EXAMPLE: The prisoners raced for the woods **when the guards turned their backs**.
The huge transport plane took off **once the maintenance crew had cleared the runway.**

Sentences that contain one independent clause and at least one dependent clause are called **complex sentences**. Dependent clauses may appear at the beginning or end of complex sentences. When the dependent clause appears at the beginning of the complex sentence, a comma is used to separate it from the independent clause.

EXAMPLE: **When the guards turned their backs,** the prisoners raced for the woods.
Once the maintenance crew had cleared the runway, the huge transport plane took off.

A. In the blanks indicate whether each sentence is simple, compound, or complex. Underline any dependent clauses you find. (You may want to return to Exercise 25 to review simple and compound sentences.)

_____ 1. Lars was just going out when the telephone rang.

_____ 2. Last year Ariel won the pie-eating contest.

_____ 3. The gun sounded, and the race began.

_____ 4. After the rain stopped, we decided to go swimming.

_____ 5. Carefully the climbers crossed the deep crevasse and scrambled up the rocky slope.

_____ 6. Whenever I try to study, I fall asleep.

_____ 7. Josh left the steaks on the table, and Adrienne's dog ate them.

_____ 8. If Kevin hits a home run, we'll win the championship.

_____ 9. The thick pads on a camel's feet keep it from sinking into the sand and protect it from the heat.

Subordinating Conjunctions and Complex Sentences (continued)

B. Each of the following word groups is a dependent clause. Make each of these clauses into a complex sentence by adding an independent clause. The dependent clause may be placed at the beginning or the end of the sentence. If the dependent clause begins the sentence, separate it from the independent clause with a comma. *Remember that the independent clause you add should make sense by itself.*

1. unless I find my key _____

_____

2. because our cat has fleas _____

_____

3. whenever Maia tries to sing _____

_____

4. although all the lights went out _____

_____

5. if Jordan mixes those two chemicals _____

_____

C. Write five complex sentences. Make sure each sentence contains one independent clause and at least one dependent clause. Underline the dependent clause in each.

_____

_____

_____

_____

_____

_____

_____

_____

_____

_____

Exercise 53 (Paragraph Construction)

Editing for Unity

As you know, a paragraph is a group of sentences about one idea, and usually this idea is stated in the topic sentence. A paragraph has **unity** when all the supporting sentences relate directly to the main idea. If any of them does not support or tie in with the main idea, the paragraph lacks unity, which can confuse a reader.

A. Below each of the following topic sentences are five details. Circle the detail that does not belong with the others and tell why.

1. Human activities are often affected by weather.
   a. sudden frosts destroy crops
   b. dark clouds indicate rain
   c. fog prevents planes from flying
   d. storms break telephone lines
   e. snow may delay trains and buses

   _____

2. As the lunar module landed, I caught my first glimpse of the moon's surface.
   a. high, jagged mountains
   b. vast, plains called seas
   c. intensely hot in daylight
   d. hundreds of craters
   e. covered with fine dust and rocks of all sizes

   _____

3. Border collies make outstanding sheep dogs.
   a. able to work long hours
   b. gentle with young lambs
   c. very intelligent dogs
   d. have long narrow heads
   e. know what to do without being told

   _____

4. The hippopotamus would never win a beauty contest.
   a. good sense of smell
   b. small beady eyes
   c. huge head with large nostrils
   d. long curved front teeth
   e. only the whale has a larger mouth

   _____

Editing for Unity (continued)

B. Read the following paragraph and identify its main idea. Then tell whether or not it has unity, and explain why.

Some of the world's most interesting animals live on the African savanna. Great herds of gazelle, antelope, zebra, and giraffe graze on the coarse grass. Meat-eaters such as lions, cheetahs, and leopards follow the herds and prey on them. Hyenas and jackals roam about, feeding on whatever the hunting animals leave after a meal. Huge herds of elephants, which have few enemies, graze on the grass, browse on low branches of trees, or pull up water plants for their food. Acacias, baobabs, and palms are some of the more common trees growing on the savanna.

Main idea: _____

_____

Does the paragraph have unity? _____

_____

C. Do you like cats? List six reasons why you do or do not like cats.

1. _____

2. _____

3. _____

4. _____

5. _____

6. _____

Now write a paragraph in your notebook using the ideas above. Be sure your topic sentence clearly expresses your feelings about cats. When you have finished, edit your work to make sure that all your sentences relate to the main idea.

Exercise 54 (Grammar and Usage)

Problem Verbs

Two verbs that often cause difficulty in English are *lie* and *lay*. Notice that the past form of the verb *lie* is the same as the present form of the verb *lay*. To avoid problems with this troublesome pair, first make sure you clearly understand their meanings. Then memorize the four principal parts of each verb.

One meaning of *lie* is "to rest or recline."

Present tense: *Lie* down if you feel tired.
Present participle: The cow is *lying* in the shade.
Past tense: Yesterday I *lay* down about noon.
Past participle: Their softball has *lain* there all day.

The verb *to lay* means "to put or place something somewhere."

Present tense: *Lay* the books on the scales.
Present participle: He is *laying* netting over the strawberries.
Past tense: She *laid* her keys beside the telephone.
Past participle: Have the workers *laid* the foundation?

Read each sentence carefully and decide whether the verb *to lie* or *to lay* is required. Then write the correct form in the blank.

1. _____ the baby carefully in the crib.

2. All last week a dense cloud of smoke _____ over the valley.

3. Is that your jacket _____ on the floor?

4. Last week the hawk _____ four eggs in the nest.

5. "Would you like to _____ down?" asked the nurse.

6. My grandmother has _____ in bed for two months.

7. The teacher closed the book, _____ it on the desk, and left the room.

8. The enormous hippopotamus was _____ half-submerged in the marsh.

9. The two cats have _____ in the sun all afternoon.

10. When they returned to the dock, the crew _____ their nets out to dry.

11. In this region, coal deposits _____ near the surface.

12. Archaeologists estimate that those bones have _____ there for five thousand years.

13. The wreck of the old galleon was _____ on a bed of coral.

14. _____ his cell phone on the park bench, the young man leaned back to enjoy a few moments of sunshine.

15. The snow has _____ in the shadow of the trees for several days.

16. The new carpet had just been _____ when Richard spilled the can of paint.

A. *Said* is a colourless verb because the action of speaking can be performed in many ways. Write five vivid verbs you could use in place of *said*. Use a thesaurus to help you.

_____

B. Write the Canadian spellings of the following words.

1. center _____

2. criticise _____

3. vigor _____

4. defense _____

C. Add parentheses, dashes, colons, semicolons, and hyphens where necessary in the following sentences.

1. To prepare for competitions, Kylie Fougere the person who won the high jump contest last year eats fruits, vegetables, and energy bars, drinks water, apple juice, and cranberry juice, and sprints, does aerobics, and lifts weights.

2. Our teacher the woman standing next to the brightly coloured van insisted that we bring three things on our class trip healthy snacks, warm clothing, and common sense.

D. In each sentence, circle the simple subject and underline the form of the verb in parentheses that agrees with the subject.

1. The pictures in this album (was, were) taken by my aunt.

2. Either two pieces of photo identification or your passport (is, are) needed at the airport.

3. Here (comes, come) your sisters now.

E. In each sentence, circle the main verb and underline helping verbs. Then, in the blanks at the right, tell whether the verb is in active voice or passive voice, and identify the tense of the verb as present, past, or future.

1. My dog was almost hit by a car yesterday. _____

2. Cathy's brother is studying law at McGill University. _____

3. The assembly will be held in the auditorium at 2:30. _____

F. Read each sentence carefully and circle the correct verb form.

1. The man had (laid, lain) his keys somewhere and could not find them now.

2. Lisa (lay, laid) awake until after midnight listening to the noise of the traffic.

3. Joaquim (lay, laid) his forehead on the steering wheel.

Review (continued)

G. Each of the following word groups is a dependent clause. Make each clause into a complex sentence by adding an independent clause. Remember to punctuate correctly.

1. when the bus finally arrived _____

_____

2. after the thunderstorm ended _____

_____

3. if the movie finished early _____

_____

H. Answer the following questions in the blanks.

Explain the purpose of a topic sentence.

_____

Tell where a writer may place a topic sentence in a paragraph, giving reasons for each placement.

_____

_____

_____

_____

_____

_____

I. On standard-sized paper write a business letter complaining about a product you recently bought. Make up names and addresses as necessary.

J. In a dictionary find each of the words in boldface type below. Read all the definitions for each entry. On the line below each sentence, write the meaning that fits best.

1. He tried to **relay** the information to the proper authorities.

_____

2. We **honour** our country's veterans on Remembrance Day.

_____

Exercise 55 (Grammar and Usage)

Adjectives

Words that modify or describe nouns or pronouns are called **adjectives**. Writers use adjectives to make the meaning of nouns more exact and to create strong impressions in their readers' minds.

> EXAMPLE: *The moose strode out into the lake.*
> *The **huge bull** moose strode out into the **cold mountain** lake.*

Adjectives tell *what kind* (**sour** milk), *how many* (**five** videos), *how much* (**some** money), *which one* (**this** cell phone), or *whose* (***my*** computer).

Usually, adjectives come before the noun or pronoun they modify. However, sometimes writers place adjectives after the noun to make them stand out.

> EXAMPLE: *The coyote, **tired** and **hungry**, searched the meadow for ground squirrels.*

Adjectives can also follow linking verbs.

> EXAMPLE: *The coyote was **tired** and **hungry**.*

Be careful not to overuse adjectives, because too many will slow down the communication of your ideas. Effective writers first try to express their ideas with specific nouns and vivid verbs; they use adjectives only when necessary to convey their meaning or mood better.

A. Circle the seventeen adjectives in the following sentences. Draw an arrow from each adjective to the noun it describes or modifies.

1. Mars is a small reddish planet with many dark patches on the surface. These patches become darker and larger during the Martian spring and summer.

2. The atmosphere on Mars is thinner and contains fewer gases than Earth's air.

3. Sometimes large areas of the planet are covered with yellow clouds, which some astronomers think are dust clouds.

4. By using powerful telescopes, scientists can see white areas at the two poles.

B. Write at least four adjectives you could use to describe each of these topics. Circle the adjective in each set you think is the most descriptive. Then, in your notebook write an interesting topic sentence for a paragraph on each subject.

> EXAMPLE: a mouse cornered by a hungry cat
> *panicky, (terrified) hysterical, petrified, frightened.*

1. a sunset on a tropical island

   _____

2. a student during a difficult examination

   _____

3. a graveyard in the morning mist

   _____

Exercise 56 (Word Skills)

Latin Roots

The **etymology** of a word means the word's origin. Etymological dictionaries usually state word origins in square brackets at the end of all the definitions, as in the following entry:

A word or a word part from which other words are formed is called a **root**, and the roots of many English words come from other languages. In fact, half of all English words have Latin roots, so learning a few common Latin roots can help you unlock the meaning of hundreds of English words. For example, knowing that the Latin root *centum* means *hundred* can help you understand the meaning of words like *centenarian* and *centenary*.

> **cen·ten·ni·al** (sĕn-tĕn′ē-əl) *adj.* **1.** Of or relating to an age or period of 100 years. **2.** Occurring once every 100 years. **3.** Of or relating to a 100th anniversary. –*n.* A 100th anniversary or a celebration of it : *Canada's centennial was celebrated in 1967.* [Lat. *centum*, hundred; see **dekm*** + (BI)ENNIAL.] – **cen·ten′ni·al·ly** *adv.*

A. Before the printing press was invented, people called *scribes* wrote books and official letters by hand. The word *scribe* comes from the Latin root *scribere* meaning "to write." Complete each of the following sentences with a word from the box below.

| describe | postscript | scribble | transcribe |
| inscription | prescription | subscribe | proscribe |

1. Something written on a tombstone is an _____

2. A note written at the end of a letter is a _____

3. If you _____ something, you write or tell what it looks like.

4. To _____ means to write carelessly.

5. The doctor wrote a _____ for some medicine.

Latin Roots (continued)

B. The root -*cide* means "to kill." Beside each word, explain who or what has been killed.

EXAMPLE: insecticide _____*insects*_____

1. pesticide_____
2. homicide _____
3. fratricide _____
4. fungicide _____
5. regicide _____

6. germicide_____
7. suicide _____
8. matricide _____
9. genocide _____
10. patricide_____

C. The words in each of the following groups are formed from the same root. On the line under each group write the root and explain what it means. Use your dictionary to help you find the root if you do not know it. Add at least one more word that comes from the same root. Make sure you know the meaning of all the words in the group.

EXAMPLE: marine   mariner   marina   submarine
          mare, meaning "the sea," maritime

1. pedestrian   biped   peddler   pedal

   _____

2. audience   auditorium   audition   audiometer

   _____

3. minicomputer   minimal   minimum   minibus

   _____

4. manuscript   manufacture   manipulate   manual

   _____

5. bisect   intersect   dissect   section

   _____

6. mortgage   mortal   immortal   morgue

   _____

7. dentist   dental   indent   trident

   _____

8. spectator   spectacular   spectre   inspector

   _____

Exercise 57 (Paragraph Construction)

Writing Clear Explanations

A good set of directions should be clear, complete, well organized, and easy to follow. Unless you know otherwise, assume that your reader knows nothing about the process you are explaining. Concentrate on providing sufficient information in an order that the reader will find easy to understand. Often the best order for directions is a sequential order, from first to last. Wherever possible, use transitional expressions like those listed in Exercise 44.

A. The following set of directions contains too many vague words and expressions, and does not include all the necessary information. In your notebook rewrite the directions, making them much more specific. Use your imagination to add details.

The nearest police station is some distance away. To get there turn at the traffic light and drive for some distance until you come to a service station. Turn north a few blocks past the service station and keep going until you come to a river. Turn here and follow the road along the river for a while. Turn again when you come to a big tree. Before long you'll see the police station. I think it's across the street from a restaurant.

B. Listed below in jumbled order are the steps required to fix a flat tire on a bicycle. On the line below the list, write the numbers of the steps in sequential order.

1. Roughen the area around the hole with sandpaper.
2. Don't use a sharp object to take the tire off the rim. You could easily damage the tire or tube.
3. To prevent further punctures, check the inside of the tire for sharp objects.
4. Stuff the rest of the tube back in the tire. Be sure it's not twisted or pinched.
5. Inflate the tire to full pressure.
6. Let all the air out of the tube.
7. Put the valve stem through the valve to hold in the rim.
8. If necessary, put the tube in water to find the leak.
9. Once the tire is on the rim, partially inflate it to make sure it fits properly.
10. Cement the patch.
11. Carefully pry the tire off the rim.
12. Locate the puncture.
13. Start at the valve when putting the tire back on the rim.

_____

C. Now use your reorganized set of directions to write a paragraph explaining how to fix a flat tire on a bicycle. Do not simply recopy the directions. To help your reader move easily from step to step, use transitional expressions such as *before you start, first, then, next,* and *last.* You will also have to add words to the directions themselves to make your sentences flow easily into one another. Be sure to begin with an effective topic sentence.

Exercise 58 (Grammar and Usage)

Adverbs

Adverbs are words that modify or describe a verb, adjective, or other adverb. When adverbs modify verbs, their job is to show *when*, *where*, or *how* something happened.

> EXAMPLE: The band from Kitsilano School arrived **yesterday**. (modifies the verb *arrived* by telling *when* the band arrived)
> The fire started **downstairs**. (modifies the verb *started* by telling *where* the fire started)
> Amy drove **skilfully** through the crowded street. (modifies the verb *drove* by telling *how* Amy drove)

When adverbs modify adjectives or other adverbs, they strengthen or intensify the adjective or adverb they modify:

> EXAMPLE: This soup is **quite** salty. (modifies the adjective *salty*)
> The river rose **very** fast. (modifies the adverb *fast*)

A. Circle the verbs and underline the adverbs in the following sentences. Above each adverb tell whether it answers the question *when*, *where*, or *how*.

> EXAMPLE: *how* Carefully they (pushed) the large box *where* outside.

1. Our volleyball team played well yesterday and easily won the tournament.

2. Sometimes the wind blows constantly.

3. Frequently the old man sat alone on the beach.

4. The school bus often arrives late.

5. My grandfather never drives fast.

B. The part of speech that a word is depends on how it is used in a sentence. In the blanks tell whether the italicized word is used as an adjective or as an adverb. Be prepared to give reasons for your choices.

1. My father often works *late* at his office. _____

2. We had a *late* breakfast on Saturday. _____

3. Lou didn't consider ten dollars a *just* price. _____

4. That apple pie is *just* delicious. _____

5. My sister doesn't feel *well* today. _____

6. Shake *well* before using. _____

7. Mr. Dobronsky always arrives *early*. _____

8. In the *early* morning there's often a mist over the lake. _____

9. Tie the boat *fast* to the dock. _____

10. Are you sure that clock is *fast*? _____

Exercise 59 (Sentence Construction)

Adverb Clauses

Adding adverbs, which explain *when*, *where*, or *how* the action in the sentence took place, helps to make your meaning clear. Often, though, you need more than a single word to explain your ideas. Whenever a clause does the job of an adverb in the sentence, it is called a dependent (or subordinate) adverb clause.

> EXAMPLE: The fireworks began **when Ms. McRae pushed the button**. (tells *when*)
> The teacher left the answers **where we could see them**. (tells *where*)
> The huge crane lifted the car from the ditch **as if it were a toy**. (tells *how*)

Adverb clauses can also be used to explain *why* something happened, or *under what conditions* something might take place.

> EXAMPLE: The plane stalled **because a fuel line froze**. (tells *why*)
> We will go **if the weather permits**. (tells *under what conditions*)

A. Underline the dependent adverb clause in each of these sentences. Draw an arrow from the dependent clause to the verb in the independent clause that it modifies. In the blank say whether the clause tells *where, when, how, why,* or *under what condition*.

EXAMPLE: Before Brent could reply, the old man slammed the door. _____*when*_____

1. As we walked home, we saw an accident on Ferguson Road._____

2. Li-Chen will go if you will. _____

3. Because it was almost dark, we hurried back to the cabin. _____

4. The elk looked as if they had not eaten for many days. _____

5. Don't move a muscle until Erin gives the signal. _____

6. As soon as I arrived home, I knew something was wrong. _____

B. In your notebook combine each of the following pairs of simple sentences by changing one sentence into an adverb clause. Be sure to begin your clause with a subordinating conjunction. Try to use as many different conjunctions as you can.

EXAMPLE: My brother won't be playing hockey this year. He broke his arm.
My brother won't be playing hockey this year because he broke his arm.

1. I forgot to clean up my room. My mother will be disappointed.
2. The teacher came into the room. He found the two boys arguing.
3. The principal announced that the school would be closed for three days. All the students cheered.
4. My sister was home before seven o'clock. The basketball game with Tupper School was cancelled.
5. Jamal was talking on the telephone. The two children ate the whole apple pie.
6. The party began at eight o'clock. Emma and Reese didn't arrive until much later.

Exercise 60 (Paragraph Construction)

Developing Paragraphs with Examples

The purpose of **expository** writing is to present a main idea and then develop or expand this idea. Often the supporting sentences develop the main idea in the topic sentence by using specific example details, which tell *how*.

A. Underline the main idea of the following paragraph and then list the examples the writer used to develop this idea.

Passenger trains in early Canada were often uncomfortable, inconvenient, and even dangerous. Joined by chains, the passenger cars started with a jerk when the train began moving. Sparks from the smokestack often set fire to the wooden passenger cars, burned holes in the passengers' clothing, and sometimes started forest fires. Frequently, locomotives did not have enough power to climb steep hills, and passengers had to get out, walk up the hill, and wait until the locomotive had built up enough steam to continue the trip.

_____

_____

_____

B. Choose one of the following topics. List at least five specific examples you could use to develop a paragraph on the topic you selected.

1. the ideal school locker
2. the many uses of wire coat hangers
3. the kitchen of the future

4. the many ways parents can embarrass teenagers
5. my relatives' strange habits

_____

_____

_____

_____

C. Using your list of examples, write a draft of your paragraph in your notebook or on a computer. Be sure to start with an effective topic sentence. Once you have written your first draft, edit your paragraph. Make sure it keeps to the topic and presents the ideas in the most effective order.

D. Use your imagination. How do you think people will travel one hundred years from now? Write a paragraph about future travel in Canada. Be sure to start with a topic sentence that will catch the reader's interest. Develop the paragraph with a series of specific examples.

Communicating Skills 8 | **77**

Proofreading

Before presenting your work to others, take time to proofread your writing for errors in grammar, spelling, punctuation, capitalization, and usage. You do not need to rewrite your paper to proofread it. Instead, use the proofreading symbols in the box below to mark the needed corrections. Use a pen that is a different colour from the colour of your writing. Once you have corrected all your errors, write a polished draft to share with your intended audience.

✘ delete	⋀ insert word or letter	˅ insert apostrophe
≡ capitalize	⋀ insert comma	¶ new paragraph
⊂ close up space	⊙ insert period	/ change to lower case
# insert space	❞ insert quotation mark	∾ transpose

A. Here is a paragraph about Canada's first astronaut, Marc Garneau. Notice how the author has used proofreading symbols to show the changes that should be made. Rewrite the paragraph below, making the changes indicated.

Canada's first astronaut was marc Garneau, a commander inthe Canadian navy and a graduate of the royal military college in Kingston. Garneau began training as an astronaut in february 1984. He spent hundreds of hours in simulators carefully rehearsing each each stage of the space shuttles flight Finally on October 5 1984 Garneau blasted off for an eight-day space mission on the space shuttle challenger. On November 30, 2000, when he launched aboard the space shuttle Endeavour, Garnau became the first Canadian to fly three space missions.

_____

_____

_____

_____

_____

_____

_____

_____

B. Select a piece you have written recently, and use the proofreading symbols to identify errors in grammar, spelling, punctuation, capitalization, and usage.

Exercise 62 (Paragraph Construction)

Developing Paragraphs with Reasons

In expository writing, often the supporting sentences develop the main idea in the topic sentence by using specific reason details, which tell *why*. Usually reasons are organized in order of importance, starting with less important reasons and ending with the most important. Transitional expressions such as *the chief factor*, *the best thing*, and *a major concern* are often used to guide the reader.

A. In the blanks below identify the main idea of the following paragraph and then list the reasons the writer used to develop this idea.

The introduction of railroads significantly changed rural Canada. With the railroad came the telegraph and the ability to communicate instantly with the rest of the world. The trains also brought city newspapers packed with up-to-date information on world events. Trips that previously took days could now be made in a matter of hours. Once the railroads were completed, manufacturers in major industrial cities in Ontario and Quebec could ship their products rapidly and economically throughout the country. Perhaps the most important change came for farmers, who could now move their goods to market quickly and cheaply.

_____

_____

_____

_____

_____

_____

B. Imagine you have just won a contest in which the prize is a three-week holiday anywhere in the world. Where would you go? Why would you choose this destination? Write a paragraph explaining where you would go. Develop your idea by giving specific reasons for your choice. Be sure to arrange your reasons in order of importance.

_____

_____

_____

_____

_____

_____

UNIT
14

Exercise 63 (Word Skills)

Greek Roots

Many English words have Greek roots. For example, the word *Cyclops*, which refers to a race of one-eyed giants in Greek mythology, is formed from two Greek roots: *kyklos*, meaning "circle," and *ops*, meaning "eye." The following are two families of English words that have grown out of these roots.

kyklos: cycle, bicycle, cyclone
ops: optical, optics, optometrist

Learning Greek roots and their families is an excellent way to improve your vocabulary, because words in a family look like one another. You can learn whole groups of words more easily if you know their common root.

A. The following group of words all share the same root—*phone*, which is the Greek word for *sound*. Using a dictionary, find the meaning of the other Greek roots in these words. Write your answers in the blanks.

1. microphone _____

2. telephone _____

3. xylophone _____

4. megaphone _____

5. homophone _____

6. phonogram _____

B. The word *meter* is from the Greek word *metron* meaning "measure." What would you use each of the following to measure?

EXAMPLE: speedometer ___*how fast something is moving*_____

1. thermometer _____

2. altimeter _____

3. pedometer _____

4. odometer _____

5. barometer _____

6. phonometer _____

Greek Roots (continued)

C. The ancient Greek words *astron* (star) and *nauta* (sailor) combine to form the modern word *astronaut*. The word *astronaut* literally means "a star sailor."

1. What is the difference between *astrology* and *astronomy*?

   _____

   _____

2. Where would you find *asteroids*?

   _____

3. When would you use an *asterisk*?

   _____

4. If people say, "That trip will cost you an *astronomical* amount," what do they mean?

   _____

UNIT 14

5. In ancient times, people believed the stars had an effect on their lives. When something like an earthquake or a flood occurred, they were sure it had happened because someone had disobeyed the will of the stars. As a result, such events became known as *disasters*—from *dis* (opposite, against) and *aster* (star). List five more words in which *dis* means *opposite* or *against*.

   _____

D. Three Greek words often found in English are *autos* (self), *bios* (life), and *graphein* (write). Use these definitions to help you work out the meaning of the following words.

1. autograph _____

   _____

2. astrobiology _____

   _____

3. automatic _____

   _____

4. biography _____

   _____

5. autobiography _____

   _____

6. autopilot _____

   _____

Exercise 64 (Grammar and Usage)

Comparison of Adjectives and Adverbs

Most adjectives and adverbs have different forms. The **positive** form is used simply to describe, not to compare. The **comparative** form is used when only two people, things, or actions are being compared. When you compare three or more things, always use the **superlative** form.

Most one-syllable adjectives and adverbs use -er to create the comparative form and -est to create the superlative form.

	Positive	**Comparative**	**Superlative**
Adjective:	long	longer	longest
Adverb:	slow	slower	slowest

Most adjectives and adverbs of two or more syllables use *more* or *most*.

	Positive	**Comparative**	**Superlative**
Adjective:	difficult	more difficult	most difficult
Adverb:	easily	more easily	most easily

A few adjectives and adverbs are irregular.

	Positive	**Comparative**	**Superlative**
Adjective:	little	less	least
Adverb:	far	farther	farthest

A few adjectives such as *dead, square, round, parallel,* and *equal* cannot be compared. Logically, if something is dead, square, round, parallel, or equal, it cannot become more dead, more square, more round, more parallel, or more equal.

A. In each of the following sentences, circle the correct form of the adjective or adverb. On the line below each sentence, explain the reason for your choice.

EXAMPLE: Of all the animals, the one with the (larger, (largest)) ears is the elephant.

more than two animals are compared

1. Which do you like (better, best), peanut butter or marmalade?

   _____

2. Which of the two bananas is the (riper, ripest)?

   _____

3. Which city is (larger, largest), Winnipeg, Saskatoon, or Edmonton?

   _____

4. Is this the (cooler, coolest) side of the street?

   _____

B. In your notebook write three sentences for each of the following adjectives. Use the adjective itself in the first sentence, its comparative form in the second, and its superlative form in the third.

hot   dangerous   heavy   sweet   good   important

Exercise 65 (Word Skills)

Other Roots

Although most English words have Latin and Greek roots, thousands have arrived from other languages as well.

EXAMPLE: tea (Chinese), *bamboo* (Malay), *kangaroo* (Australian Aboriginal language)

As English settlers moved westward across North America, they frequently borrowed words from First Nations languages to describe the animals and plants they had not seen before.

EXAMPLE: skunk, moose, opossum, squash, hickory

Immigrants who came to North America from other countries also introduced new words to the English language. From France came *cache* and *prairie*; from Spain came *bronco* and *corral*; from Holland came *cookie* and *caboose*; from Germany came *hamburger* and *noodle*; and from Italy came *pizza* and *spaghetti*.

Underline the correct word to complete the sentence about each italicized word, and in the blanks identify the language from which the word was borrowed. Use a dictionary if you are unsure of the answers.

1. A *tango* is a kind of (a) monkey, (b) drum, (c) dance, (d) racing car. _____

2. To play *polo* you need (a) a gymnasium, (b) a checker board, (c) ice skates, (d) a fast horse. _____

3. A *ukulele* is (a) a musical instrument, (b) a song, (c) a large parrot, (d) a bullfighter. _____

4. You wear a *fez* on your (a) feet, (b) hands, (c) shoulders, (d) head. _____

5. If you took lessons in *jujitsu* you would learn to (a) speak Chinese, (b) defend yourself, (c) cook, (d) sail a boat. _____

6. If something is *taboo* it is (a) good to eat, (b) very colourful, (c) not allowed, (d) unknown. _____

7. At a *smorgasbord* people usually (a) watch television, (b) trade stamps, (c) eat, (d) buy lumber. _____

8. A *sauna* is (a) a steam bath, (b) a heavy rainfall, (c) a small lizard, (d) a short song. _____

9. A *chinook* is (a) a type of fish hook, (b) a warm wind, (c) a fast-flowing stream, (d) a fog or mist. _____

10. *Azure* is the colour of (a) a lump of coal, (b) maple leaves in the fall, (c) the clear sky, (d) an African elephant's hide. _____

UNIT
15

Communicating Skills 8 | 83

Exercise 66 (Composition Construction)

Persuasive Writing

Persuasive writing is writing that gets things done. It moves readers to believe something or to act in a certain way. A persuasive essay or article often begins with a statement of the author's position, then presents arguments and evidence in favour of that position, and concludes with a call to action or a recommendation. Persuasive writers arrange their points in a way that best suits their argument, often saving their strongest arguments until last.

Although persuasive essays may appeal to a reader's emotions, the most effective essays are those that offer facts and logical arguments to support their position. Also, skilful writers anticipate negative responses and offer counterarguments to diminish their significance. For example, if a reader might argue that cost would prohibit the building of a community skateboard park, the writer anticipates this and suggests realistic ways the community might raise the necessary funds.

A. In the blanks below, brainstorm a list of issues about which you feel strongly. These might be issues relating to your school (e.g., the need for a student lounge), your community (e.g., the need for a local food bank); your country (e.g., the need for better health care); or the world (e.g., the need to reduce greenhouse gas emissions). Generate as many issues as you can. If possible, look through your journal for ideas you might write about.

_____

_____

_____

_____

_____

_____

B. The best issues are those about which you feel most strongly. Look at the list you brainstormed above and put check marks beside those that evoke the strongest reactions in you. From these, choose one that you know the most about and could develop into a persuasive essay. In the blank below write the issue you have chosen.

_____

C. In the space below state the purpose of your essay by deciding exactly what you want to convince your reader to believe or to do.

_____

_____

Persuasive Writing (continued)

D. In the space below jot down as many arguments as you can think of to persuade your reader to support your position. Do not worry about whether the arguments make sense right now—the important thing is to record as many ideas as possible. Write in point form so you can record your ideas quickly.

_____

_____

_____

_____

E. In the space below jot down as many arguments as you can think of that readers might use to attack your position.

_____

_____

_____

_____

_____

UNIT 15

F. After each argument you listed in Activity E, jot down a counterargument that you could use to diminish its significance. If you have listed arguments that you cannot counter, you may have to conduct some research to find evidence that will support you.

G. Look at the arguments you have identified. Choose three or four of your strongest points and write them in your notebook. Be sure to include at least one or two of the counterarguments you have developed. Decide whether you need to do further research to find facts that will support your position.

H. Once you are satisfied with your arguments and your supporting information, decide on an order to present your arguments. An effective persuasive essay ends with its strongest argument since that will be the one the reader will remember most. However, be sure to begin with a strong argument, too.

I. Write a draft of your persuasive essay in your notebook. Begin with a statement or image that will arouse your reader's interest, and state your position clearly. Be sure to discuss each argument fully in a separate paragraph. Conclude your essay by restating your position in different words and making it clear how your reader will benefit from adopting or agreeing with your position.

Exercise 67 (Word Skills)

Building Words with Prefixes

A **prefix** is a word part added to the beginning of a root to change its meaning. Understanding the meaning of some of the more common prefixes will improve your vocabulary. For example, knowing that *pre-* means "before" would help you recognize *prearrange* (to arrange beforehand) or *prepay* (to pay in advance).

Adding a prefix changes the meaning of the root word. If the new word means the opposite of the root word, it is called an **antonym**.

EXAMPLE:	Root Word	Prefix	New Word	New Meaning
	certain	un-	uncertain	not certain
	appear	re-	reappear	appear again

A. Circle the prefix in each of these words.

1. inexpensive
2. disagreeable
3. misspelled
4. nonsmoking
5. rearrange
6. unexpected
7. overcooked
8. displease

B. Form the antonym of each of the words listed below by adding the prefix *un-*, *in-*, *il-*, *im-*, or *ir-*. Use your dictionary if you are not sure which prefix is correct.

1. fair _____
2. legible _____
3. sane _____
4. reversible _____
5. pure _____
6. certain _____
7. correct _____
8. measurable _____
9. religious _____
10. polite _____

11. logical_____
12. responsible _____
13. replaceable _____
14. proper _____
15. happy _____
16. literate _____
17. flexible_____
18. known _____
19. complete _____
20. usual_____

Building Words with Prefixes (continued)

C. In your notebook use prefixes to make one or more new words from each of the following root words. Use a dictionary to be sure that the words you form do exist.

arrange   copy   fit   judge   read   shape   use   print   change   address   test   count   heat

D. Each pair of words in the following chart has a common prefix. In the second column write the common prefix and its meaning. In the third column write two additional words that have the same prefix. Use a dictionary if necessary. When you have completed the chart, write sentences in your notebook using each word in the third column correctly.

Word Pairs	Common Prefix	Additional Words
1. supernatural supersonic		
2. subway submarine		
3. anti-aircraft antifreeze		
4. reappear review		
5. semiconscious semicircle		
6. postwar postscript		
7. preheat prefabricate		
8. foretold forehead		
9. nonfiction nonsmoking		
10. misbehave misunderstand		
11. multicoloured multimillionaire		
12. overslept overpaid		

Exercise 68 (Grammar and Usage)

Pronouns

A **pronoun** is a word that takes the place of one or more nouns. The word or group of words that a pronoun replaces or refers to is called its **antecedent**.

> EXAMPLE: The greatest speed skater in Canadian history is Gaetan Boucher. He won a silver and two gold medals at the 1984 Olympic Games.

The antecedent of the pronoun *he,* in the second sentence, is the noun *Gaetan Boucher.* Personal pronouns are the most commonly used pronouns. First-person pronouns are used by speakers to refer to themselves (*I, me, we, us, my, mine, our, ours*). Second-person pronouns refer to the person spoken to (*you, your, yours*). Third-person pronouns refer to the person or thing spoken about (*she, her, hers, he, him, his, it, its, one, they, them, their, theirs*).

On the line below each of the following sentences, write the personal pronouns found in that sentence. After each pronoun write its antecedent.

EXAMPLE: Andrew folded the pants carefully and packed them in his suitcase.

them - pants   his - Andrew

1. José spent an hour looking for his glasses, but he couldn't find them.

   _____

2. Lynne asked her parents to wake her up when they got home.

   _____

3. Gillian asked her cousin if he could come for dinner on Sunday.

   _____

4. "Did you give the puppies their supper, Shay?" asked Mr. Kolchinsky.

   _____

5. Marie brought her uniform home, but Marla and Caitlin left theirs at school.

   _____

6. "Ms. Joleski has a pair of scissors, Maura. She will let you borrow them."

   _____

7. "I left your music books on the table so you wouldn't forget them, Matt," said Mr. Yamada.

   _____

8. Fazal couldn't go to the football game with the Browns because their car wouldn't start.

   _____

Exercise 69 (Punctuation and Capitalization)

Using Apostrophes to Show Possession

Nouns that show who or what something belongs to are called **possessive nouns**. We use **apostrophes** to show possession. To make a singular noun possessive, add an apostrophe followed by an -s.

EXAMPLE: Where is the **dog's** leash?

To form the possessive of a plural noun ending in -s, simply add an apostrophe.

EXAMPLE: the **carpenters'** tools   the **players'** plane tickets

To form the possessive of a plural noun that does not end in -s, add an apostrophe and -s.

EXAMPLE: the **women's** dresses   the **children's** playground

When something is owned jointly by two or more people, make only the final noun possessive.

EXAMPLE: **Paulo and Bret's** science project won first prize.

When the ownership of something is separate, make both nouns possessive.

EXAMPLE: The **Browns'** and the **Smiths'** children attended the same school.

With compound nouns, add an apostrophe and -s to the final part of the expression.

EXAMPLE: my **father-in-law's** car   the **bird-watcher's** binoculars

A. Rewrite each of the following word groups, using apostrophes.

EXAMPLE: the Porsche belonging to Ms. Leung _____Ms. Leung's Porsche_____

1. the shovel belonging to Mr. Peters_____

2. the blankets of the babies _____

3. the testimony of the witnesses _____

4. the farm belonging to his son-in-law _____

5. the classroom of the grade five students _____

6. the roots of the rose bushes _____

7. the parrot belonging to Tamika and Marcus _____

8. a holiday of six months _____

B. In your notebook rewrite each of the following phrases, making the italicized possessive noun plural.

EXAMPLE: the *army's* flag _____the armies' flag_____

1. the *wolf's* tracks
2. the *chief justice's* decision
3. the *city's* residents
4. the *calf's* bawling
5. the *soprano's* singing

6. the *tomato's* seeds
7. the *guppy's* fins
8. his *son-in-law's* truck
9. the *mongoose's* teeth
10. the *major general's* uniform

Communicating Skills 8

Number Prefixes

Many English words use Greek and Latin number words as prefixes. Knowing Greek and Latin prefixes can help you to understand the English words that use them. For example, the prefix *tri-*, used in words such as *tricycle* and *triple*, is from the Latin *tres*, meaning "three." The Greek word *pente*, meaning "five," is used as a prefix in such words as *pentagon* (a five-sided figure) and *pentathlon* (an athletic contest with five events).

A. In the following chart the most common number prefixes in English are listed along with their meanings. In the third column write at least two words using each prefix.

Number	Prefix	Examples
one	mono-, uni-	
two	bi-, duo-, dua-	
three	tri-	
four	quad-, quat-, quart-	
five	quint-, penta-, pent-	
six	hexa-, hex-, sex-	
seven	sept-	
eight	octa-, octo-	
nine	novem-, non-	
ten	dec-, deca-	
hundred	cent-, centi-	

B. Each word in the box contains a number prefix. The list is in alphabetical order. Rewrite the words in numerical order below.

bimonthly	decathlon	November	quartet	September
centennial	monorail	octopus	quintet	trisect

_____   _____

_____   _____

_____   _____

_____   _____

_____   _____

Number Prefixes (continued)

C. Write a sentence using each of the following words. In your sentence, include a number that helps define the word. Use a dictionary if you're unsure of a word's meaning.

EXAMPLE: quintet _A quintet is a group of five musicians._

1. trilogy _____

_____

2. centurion _____

_____

3. sextuplet _____

_____

4. bilingual _____

5. unilateral _____

6. duet _____

D. Sometimes words appear as though they begin with a prefix when they actually do not. Each of the following word groups contains a word that looks as though it begins with a number prefix, but does not. Write the word that has no prefix in the blank at the right.

EXAMPLE: octopus oculist octave octagon_____ _oculist_ _____

1. centipede centigrade centurion centralize _____

2. decade decipher decimal decimate _____

3. trisect triceps trio tribute _____

4. biology bisect biweekly biennial _____

5. quintet quinine quintuplet quinquennial _____

E. Write interesting sentences in your notebook, using each of the words you have written in the blanks above.

Exercise 71 (Punctuation and Capitalization)

Further Uses of Apostrophes

Apostrophes have other uses besides showing possession.
1. An apostrophe shows which letters have been omitted in contractions. A **contraction** is two words shortened into one.
   EXAMPLE: they've, he'll, aren't

   Contractions are often used to join a verb with the word *not*. Usually you shorten *not* to *n't* and join it to the verb.
   EXAMPLE: is + not = isn't   was + not = wasn't   did + not = didn't

   This rule has two exceptions:
   EXAMPLE: can + not = can't   will + not = won't

2. Use an apostrophe to show the omission of a number from a date.
   EXAMPLE: Back in '83, my grandparents bought a farm near Stratford.

3. Use an apostrophe and *-s* to form the plural of letters.
   EXAMPLE: Does he spell his last name with two **t's**?
   Marika usually gets **A's** on her tests.

4. Do not use an apostrophe to form the plural of numbers.
   EXAMPLE: My uncle spent the **1980s** in Japan.

Rewrite these sentences, adding apostrophes where necessary.

1. Youll probably find Jacks key in the top drawer.

   _____

2. Lets meet again in three days time.

   _____

3. The Winter Olympics were held in Calgary in 88.

   _____

4. The judges decision wont be announced until Friday.

   _____

5. Ericas reference books are more up-to-date than Ethans.

   _____

6. Tonights game is the Blue Jays against the Oakland As.

   _____

7. I wouldve preferred chocolate.

   _____

8. Theyd planned to meet Ashleys cousin at the airport.

   _____

Exercise 72 (Sentence Construction)

Complex Sentences with Adjective Clauses

Adding adjectives and adjective clauses to a sentence gives readers more exact information. Note the difference between the information in the following sentences:

The book belongs to Antonio.

*The **science** book **that you borrowed** belongs to Antonio.*

(adjective)   (adjective clause)

Subordinate adjective clauses do the work of adjectives by making the noun they modify more exact. Adjective clauses always begin with the word *who, whom, whose, which,* or *that.* These words are called **relative pronouns** because they relate, or connect, the adjective clause to the noun or pronoun it modifies.

Combine each of the following pairs of sentences by changing the italicized sentence into an adjective clause. Underline the adjective clause in your revised sentence and draw an arrow to the noun or pronoun it modifies. Be sure to start your clause with a relative pronoun and place it directly after the noun or pronoun to which it refers.

EXAMPLE: The man missed the train. *He was reading a newspaper.*

The man who was reading a newspaper missed the train.

1. Mrs. Woitzik owned the drugstore. *It burned down last night.*

2. More than thirty volunteers are still searching the mountain for the two skiers. *They disappeared last Sunday.*

3. George Reed set forty-four Canadian Football League records. *He played for the Saskatchewan Roughriders from 1962 to 1975.*

4. The small village of Snag recorded the lowest official temperature ever measured in Canada on February 3, 1947. *Snag is located 465 km northwest of Whitehorse.*

5. Prince William was born in 1982. *He is heir to the British throne.*

UNIT
17

Exercise 73 (Grammar and Usage)

Restrictive and Nonrestrictive Clauses

Restrictive clauses are clauses that restrict the meaning of the nouns they describe by identifying exactly who or what is being discussed. Restrictive clauses are essential to the sentence. **Nonrestrictive clauses** simply provide additional information and are not essential to the sentence. Nonrestrictive clauses are separated from the rest of the sentence with commas.

> *Example:* The man **who lost his wallet** is waiting in the office. *(restrictive clause)*
> Lester B. Pearson, **who was a former Olympic hockey player and university professor,** became prime minister of Canada in 1963. *(nonrestrictive clause)*

When using the relative pronouns *that* or *which*, use *that* with restrictive clauses and *which* with nonrestrictive clauses.

> *Example:* The house that burned down was on Shaw Road. *(restrictive clause)*
> The new movie, which is a comedy, opens on Tuesday. *(nonrestrictive clause)*

A. Combine each of the following sentences by changing the second sentence into an adjective clause. Underline the adjective clause in your revised sentence, and draw an arrow to the noun or pronoun it modifies. Be sure to start your clause with a relative pronoun. Place it directly after the noun or pronoun to which it refers. If the clause is nonrestrictive, be sure to separate it from the rest of the sentence with commas.

EXAMPLE: Drumheller's Tyrrell Museum is one of the largest paleontological museums in the world. It was the first Canadian institution devoted entirely to the study of fossils.

Drumheller's Tyrrell Museum, which was the first Canadian institution devoted entirely to the study of fossils, is one of the largest paleontological museums in the world.

1. The Columbia Icefield feeds the North Saskatchewan, Columbia, Athabasca, and Fraser rivers. This ice field is located on the British Columbia–Alberta border.

   _____

   _____

   _____

2. Arthur Erickson is one of Canada's best-known architects. He designed Simon Fraser University in Burnaby, the Bank of Canada building in Ottawa, and Roy Thomson Hall in Toronto.

   _____

   _____

   _____

Restrictive and Nonrestrictive Clauses (continued)

B. Expand each of the following simple sentences by adding clauses according to the directions in brackets. Underline the new clause in your revised sentence.

EXAMPLE: We finally reached the top of the mountain. (*Add an adverb clause telling when.*)

As the sun was setting, we finally reached the top of the mountain.

1. Angelo scored fifteen points in last night's basketball game. (*Add an adjective clause describing Angelo.*)

2. Yoshio and I didn't get to school until eleven o'clock. (*Add an adverb clause explaining why.*)

3. That bottle must always be kept tightly sealed. (*Add a second independent clause to make a compound sentence.*)

4. Erin burst into the room. (*Add an adverb clause telling how.*)

5. Trudy carefully opened the small package. (*Add an adjective clause describing the package.*)

6. Rolf tried desperately to prevent the tank from exploding. (*Add a second independent clause to make a compound sentence.*)

UNIT
17

Exercise 74 (Grammar and Usage)

Prepositions

A **preposition** is a word that shows the relationship between a noun or pronoun and another word in the sentence.

> EXAMPLE: The kittens played **in** the basket, **beside** the basket, and **on** the basket.

The words *in*, *beside*, and *on* are prepositions. These words show where the kittens were in relation to the basket. The following are some common prepositions:

about	at	by	into	outside	under
above	before	down	like	over	underneath
across	behind	during	near	past	until
after	below	except	of	since	up
against	beneath	for	off	through	upon
along	beside	from	on	throughout	with
among	between	in	onto	to	within
around	beyond	inside	out	toward	without

A group of words that begins with a preposition and ends with a noun or a pronoun is called a **prepositional phrase**. The noun or a pronoun at the end of a prepositional phrase is called the object of the preposition. This word usually answers the question *what* or *whom*.

> EXAMPLE: **During the winter** most bears hibernate. (during what?)
> Did Danielle leave **with him**? (with whom?)

Prepositional phrases are used to make nouns and verbs more precise. A phrase that gives additional information about a noun is called an adjective phrase.

> EXAMPLE: *The plane landed.*
> *The plane **with a damaged wing** landed.*

Prepositional phrases that tell *when*, *where*, or *how* an action took place are called adverb phrases.

> EXAMPLE: *The plane with a damaged wing landed **around six o'clock**.* (tells when)
> *The plane with a damaged wing landed **on the frozen lake**.* (tells where)
> *The plane with a damaged wing landed **without an accident**.* (tells how)

A. In each blank, write a prepositional adjective phrase that will help to identify the noun in boldface type. Be sure your phrase starts with a preposition and ends with a noun or pronoun.

EXAMPLE: The **monkey** _with the dog-like face_ keeps scratching its forehead.

1. My music teacher is the **woman** _____.

2. We saw a black bear on the **trail** _____.

3. The **skateboards** _____ have all been sold.

4. Our **relatives** _____ will be staying for six weeks.

5. The **trip** _____ could be dangerous.

6. Malcolm's **notebook** _____ is missing.

7. I prefer the **shirt** _____.

Prepositions (continued)

B. Write interesting sentences using each of these prepositional phrases as an adjective phrase. Be sure to place the phrase immediately after the noun or pronoun it modifies.

1. in the school parking lot _____

   _____

2. around the piano _____

   _____

3. along the river bank _____

   _____

4. under the principal's chair _____

   _____

5. between the two wrestlers _____

   _____

6. through the rapids _____

   _____

C. Complete the following sentences by adding prepositional adverb phrases according to the directions.

1. We found the strange trinket _____. (tell where)

2. The angry moose swam across the lake _____. (tell how)

3. _____ (tell when) our English teacher is usually in a good mood.

4. To avoid waking my parents, I closed the door _____. (tell how)

5. _____ (tell where) came a hairy turtle-like creature.

6. When the hikers finally reached the end of the trail, they pitched their tents

   _____. (tell where)

7. _____ the house next door caught fire. (tell when)

8. Clouds of thick smoke billowed _____

   (tell how) from the upper floor.

Making Pronouns Agree

If the **antecedent** of a personal pronoun is singular, the pronoun must also be singular. If the antecedent is plural, the pronoun must be plural. Unlike personal pronouns, **indefinite pronouns** do not have a definite antecedent. Instead, indefinite pronouns refer to an unnamed person or thing.

EXAMPLE: Did **anyone** turn off the lights?

Some indefinite pronouns are always singular.

Singular indefinite pronouns

anybody	*anyone*	*anything*	*each*	*either*
everybody	*everyone*	*everything*	*neither*	*nobody*
no one	*one*	*somebody*	*someone*	

Some indefinite pronouns are always plural.

Plural indefinite pronouns

both	*few*	*many*	*several*

With indefinite pronouns, it is often difficult to know whether to use the feminine pronoun *her* or the masculine pronoun *his*. Sometimes, the answer is obvious.

EXAMPLE: **Each** of the girls passed **her** test.

At other times, however, you cannot know whether the indefinite pronoun refers to males or females. In such cases, use both.

EXAMPLE: **Everyone** on the basketball team played **his or her** best.

Each of these sentence uses an indefinite pronoun as the simple subject. Circle each simple subject. Write S over the subject if it is singular and P if it is plural. Then write the pronoun that correctly completes each sentence in the blank.

EXAMPLE: (One) of the girls injured (her, their) wrist. _____ *her* _____

1. Neither of the drivers admitted that (he or she, they) was at fault. _____

2. Everyone has (her or his, their) own ideas on how to train a dog. _____

3. Neither of the cats would eat (its, their) food. _____

4. Several students forgot to bring (her or his, their) bus passes. _____

5. Has anyone in the class finished (his or her, their) history project? _____

6. Many of the geese had (its, their) wings clipped. _____

7. Each of the students could invite two of (her or his, their) friends. _____

8. If anyone phones, please tell (her or him, them) I'll be home by six. _____

9. One of the volleyball players left (her or his, their) cell phone behind. _____

10. Both cooks are taking (his or her, their) holidays this month. _____

11. Nobody is allowed inside unless (he or she, they) has a security pass. _____

12. Each of the salespeople uses (his or her, their) own car. _____

Exercise 76 (Word Skills)

Creating New Words with Suffixes

A word part added to the end of a root word to form a new word with a different meaning or function is called a **suffix**. Like prefixes, a few suffixes, such as *-less*, can change the meaning of the root word.

EXAMPLE: hope – hopeless   care – careless   end – endless

Unlike prefixes, however, many suffixes can change a root word from one part of speech to another. Some suffixes, such as *-ance*, *-ment*, *-er*, *-ness*, and *-tion* change verbs into nouns.

EXAMPLE: disappear (verb) + ance = disappearance (noun)

Sometimes the spelling of the root word changes when the suffix is added.

EXAMPLE: admire + tion = admiration   evaporate + tion = evaporation

Some suffixes change nouns into adjectives.

EXAMPLE: success (noun) + ful = successful (adjective)

Adjectives can also be made from verbs by adding the suffixes *-ing* or *-able*.

EXAMPLE: excite (verb) + ing = exciting (adjective)

As well as making new nouns and adjectives, suffixes can also be added to many adjectives to form verbs.

EXAMPLE: damp (adjective)+ en = dampen (verb)
winter (noun) + ize = winterize (verb)

A. In each of the following sentences, create adjectives by adding one of the suffixes in the box to the italicized word. Check the spelling of the new word in the dictionary.

-ous	-ance	-able	-ful	-less	-ish	-ive	-ate

EXAMPLE: Because he constantly made a *fool* of himself, people considered him _foolish_.

1. When you *consider* other people's feelings, you are being _____.

2. Something that you *use* frequently is _____.

3. Insects that *destroy* crops are _____.

4. Anyone who *attends* regularly will receive an _____ award.

5. A person who is without *guilt* is _____.

6. A child who is always getting into *mischief* is _____.

B. The noun suffixes *-ist*, *-eer*, *-er*, and *-or* all mean "a person who does something." A *teacher*, for example, is "a person who teaches." Add suffixes to change each of the following verbs into nouns meaning "a person who." Be sure to use your dictionary if you are unsure of the answer.

1. votes   _____

2. plays piano   _____

3. defects   _____

4. announces   _____

5. prospects   _____

6. auctions   _____

UNIT
18

Exercise 77 (Grammar and Usage)

Pronoun Case

Personal pronouns have different forms, or cases, depending on whether they are subjects or objects in a sentence. These **subjective case** pronouns act as subjects in sentences: *I, he, she, it, we, you, one, they.* Use the subjective case when a pronoun replaces a noun that is the subject of the sentence.

> EXAMPLE: ***Ellen** has a large collection of Swedish stamps.*
> ***She** has a large collection of Swedish stamps.*

You may have trouble deciding which form of the pronoun to use, however, if the subject is compound. To decide which pronoun is correct, read the sentence as if each pronoun stood by itself.

> EXAMPLE: *Noah and (I, me) put the volleyball net away.*
> ***I** put the volleyball net away.*
> ***Noah and I** put the volleyball net away.*

These **objective case** pronouns act as objects in sentences: *me, him, her, it, us, you, them.* Use the objective case when the pronoun follows an action verb and answers the question *whom* or *what.*

> EXAMPLE: *The large bumblebee stung **Nathan** on the leg. (stung whom?)*
> *The large bumblebee stung **him** on the leg.*

Use the objective case when the pronoun is the object of a preposition. A prepositional phrase begins with a preposition and ends with the object of a preposition.

> EXAMPLE: *Natalie usually agrees with Jenna and **me**.*
> *Between you and **me**, I'm sure we can find the answer.*

Personal pronouns are often used in sentences containing comparisons. Choosing the right pronoun is not difficult if you always remember to complete the comparison.

> EXAMPLE: *Christy went home earlier than (we, us).*

To decide which pronoun to use, mentally fill in the words that have been left out.

> EXAMPLE: *Christy went home earlier than **we** (went home).*
> *That jacket fits you better than (it fits) **me**.*

A. Decide whether each of the following word groups contains subjective case or objective case pronouns. Then, in your notebook write interesting sentences of your own, using each word group correctly.

1. Uncle Brad and him

2. Scott and I

3. her and me

4. Paulo and us

5. Erica, Travis, and they

6. my younger brother and him

7. she and Cecille

8. you and her

9. Devin or me

10. him and me

Pronoun Case (continued)

B. Write the correct pronouns in the blanks at the right. Test each sentence by reading it without the noun and the word *and*.

1. Samantha and (I, me) can't leave until noon. _____

2. We met Caleb and (he, him) in Cardston. _____

3. Olivia and (they, them) are going to the hockey game. _____

4. Did you remember to invite Jamal and (she, her)? _____

5. Alicia and (she, her) are often late. _____

6. My grandparents sent Connor and (he, him) a postcard. _____

7. We saw Pardeep and (they, them) near Smith's Pharmacy. _____

8. My brother is helping Lynn and (I, me). _____

9. The team from Southland and (they, them) were on the same bus. _____

10. Chen didn't tell Antonio and (I, me) about the meeting. _____

11. Sandy gave the cassette tapes to Karla and (I, me). _____

12. Those letters are for Adam and (he, him). _____

13. Mr. Lopez wants Erin and (she, her) to be on the relay team. _____

C. Write the correct form of the pronoun in the blank at the right. Test each sentence by completing the comparison in your mind.

1. Maya is almost as tall as (he, him). _____

2. That colour suits you better than (I, me). _____

3. Mr. Araki enjoyed the trip as much as (we, us). _____

4. Do you really think Chad is stronger than (I, me)? _____

5. You know more about raising budgies than (they, them). _____

6. Winning the trophy is more important for Josh than (I, me). _____

7. Beth is a faster skater than (she, her). _____

8. Mrs. Adams paid Pia more than (I, me). _____

9. Do you think anyone will be later than (we, us)? _____

10. Shopping for birthday presents takes me much longer than (she, her). _____

UNIT
18

Combining Sentences with Prepositional Phrases

Writers often combine a number of short sentences by using prepositional phrases.

EXAMPLE: *The winning team ate 220 pickled onions. They were from Prince Albert, Saskatchewan. They finished the onions in two minutes.*

The winning team, **from Prince Albert, Saskatchewan,** *ate 220 pickled onions* **in two minutes.**

In each of the following groups of sentences, use the first sentence as a base. Change the other two sentences into prepositional phrases, and combine them with the first sentence.

1. Mr. Littlewood cut the lawn. He cut the lawn after lunch. He used his new lawn mower.

   _____

   _____

2. Last night I found a wallet. I found it near Astorino's Restaurant. The wallet had the initials "M.E.D." on it.

   _____

   _____

3. The boy keeps us awake. He has a trumpet. He lives in the house next door.

   _____

   _____

4. The stamps are mine. They are in a small brown envelope. The envelope is in the top drawer of my dresser.

   _____

   _____

5. My younger sister is taking skiing lessons. She has lessons Saturday mornings. Her instructor is André Moser.

   _____

   _____

6. The large trailer truck skidded and crashed into the bridge. It had a load of lumber. It skidded on the wet pavement.

   _____

   _____

A. The words in each of the following groups are formed from the same root. Beside each group write the root and explain what it means. Add one more word that comes from the same root.

graphite, graphic, graphology _____

microscope, macroscopic, stethoscope _____

B. Form the antonym of each of the words listed below by adding the prefix *un-*, *in-*, *il-*, *im-*, or *ir-*.

movable _____   reconcilable_____

legal _____   correct _____

C. Add apostrophes where necessary in the following sentences.

1. The Toronto Blue Jays won the World Series in 92 and 93.
2. Shell wait for Mikes parents at the train station.
3. When writing, dont forget to dot your is.
4. Were planning to see the film in four days time.

D. Use commas where necessary to separate nonrestrictive clauses from the rest of the sentence. If the sentence has no nonrestrictive clauses, write N in the blank.

_____ 1. The officer who saved the drowning child received a medal for bravery.

_____ 2. Tisha Rowling who won the relay race yesterday is a favourite to win the long-distance competition today.

_____ 3. My wristwatch which is quite old keeps good time.

_____ 4. The prize that Jeremy won is a computer game.

E. Tell whether each italicized word is used as an adjective, adverb, or preposition.

1. We *only* designed the project. _____

2. Greg was the *only* person in the office. _____

3. The prisoner has not been seen *since.* _____

4. Tiffany has been absent *since* Tuesday. _____

F. In each of the following sentences, circle the correct form of the modifier.

1. This movie is the (better, best) of the two rentals.
2. Which of the three sisters is the (older, oldest)?

UNITS
12–18

Review (continued)

G. Underline each pronoun in these sentences and draw an arrow to its antecedent.

1. Gillian gave Daniel the book he wanted.

2. Shay asked his parents if they would chaperone the dance.

3. Marcia brought an extra jacket but Tim left his at home.

H. Write the correct pronoun in each blank.

1. Neither of the students had done (his or her, their) homework. _____

2. Each of the boys spent (his or her, their) money on snacks. _____

3. Several parents volunteered (her or his, their) time to work on prom decorations. _____

4. One of the five cats had (its, their) front claws clipped today. _____

5. Brad and (I, me) have been practising for the concert every night. _____

6. They met Lorenzo and (her, she) at the mall. _____

7. You completed the task faster than (he, him). _____

I. Tell whether each boldface group of words is an adjective clause, an adverb clause, or a prepositional phrase.

1. They planned to meet in the park **beside the skateboard ramp**. _____

2. **After the dance ended**, the musicians ordered take-out pizza. _____

3. I got back the test **that we wrote on Wednesday**. _____

J. Write a paragraph offering at least three reasons why teachers should not give tests on Mondays.

_____

_____

_____

_____

_____

_____

Exercise 79 (Study Skills)

Using Thesaurus Software

Most word-processing programs include thesaurus applications that allow writers to find synonyms and antonyms with a few key strokes, which can be much faster than using a print thesaurus. However, writers must still be careful to check the meaning of the synonyms they choose, because different synonyms have different shades of meaning. (See Exercise 23 for further discussion of synonyms and thesauri.)

Using the same words repeatedly can make writing sound boring. Along with the thesaurus application, writers can also use the Find command that appears on the drop-down Edit menu in most word-processing programs. The Find command will locate all the uses of a word in a document, which can help writers to determine whether they have overused certain words. To avoid repetition, they can use the thesaurus application to replace them with appropriate synonyms.

Besides using thesaurus applications to avoid repetition, writers also use them to replace general nouns and colourless verbs, which do not create strong impressions, with specific nouns and vivid verbs. (See Exercise 22 and Exercise 43 for further discussion of specific nouns and vivid verbs.)

A. Use the thesaurus application of your word-processing program to find synonyms for the following words. In the blanks, list as many of the synonyms your thesaurus offers for each word as possible.

1. trouble (noun) _____

_____

2. angry (adjective) _____

_____

3. leave (verb) _____

_____

B. Use a print thesaurus to find synonyms for the three words in Activity A, and list them in your notebook. Which thesaurus, the print or the computer, was more helpful?

C. The following passage contains general nouns and colourless verbs that do not create strong impressions. Scan it—or type it—into a word-processing program and use your thesaurus application to replace these words with specific nouns and vivid verbs. Highlight the synonyms you used and print a hard copy of your revised passage and place it in your notebook.

UNIT
19

The man opened the door of the room and looked inside. He stood in the doorway for a time and then entered the room and walked over to the furniture near the wall. The man sat on the furniture, then stood up and took an object from his clothing. He moved across the room to the thing in the corner. He touched it and then laughed.

Exercise 80 (Sentence Construction)
Sentence Problems: Fragments, Comma Splices, and Run-On Sentences

Writers must be able to recognize and correct three kinds of sentence problems: sentence fragments, comma splices, and run-on sentences. A **sentence fragment** is a part of a sentence that is punctuated as if it were a complete sentence.

> EXAMPLE: *When Chinese immigrants first arrived in Canada.*
> *At the beginning of the Fraser River gold rush in British Columbia.*

A **comma splice** occurs when the writer joins two complete thoughts with a comma. A comma cannot join; it only separates.

> EXAMPLE: *Chinese immigrants were instrumental in uniting Canadians, their work on the transcontinental railway helped connect the country's population and industry.*

A **run-on sentence** occurs when the writer writes two complete thoughts as one sentence without joining the thoughts with a conjunction or a form of punctuation such as a semicolon or a dash.

> EXAMPLE: *Between 1881 and 1885 more than 15 000 Chinese arrived in Canada most of the newcomers came to help build the Canadian Pacific Railway.*

A. Read the following sentences and decide whether they are written correctly or if they contain errors in sentence structure. If a sentence is correct, put a check mark in the blank. If a sentence is a fragment, a comma splice, or a run-on sentence, write F, CS, or RO in the blank.

_____ 1. After the train left the station.

_____ 2. Because my watch had stopped, I missed the bus.

_____ 3. A cat crossed the road in front of Jim's car, he had to slam on the brakes.

_____ 4. Harrison bought new sneakers he will run in a marathon this weekend.

_____ 5. Hurrying along the crowded street toward the bus stop.

_____ 6. The deer stopped and sniffed the air; smoke drifted across the meadow.

_____ 7. All of the twenty-four children in the classroom.

_____ 8. Before the movie ended, several people stood and moved toward the exit.

_____ 9. We wrote two tests and a quiz today, our teachers were preparing us for exams.

_____ 10. Go now.

Sentence Problems: Fragments, Comma Splices, and Run-On Sentences (continued)

B. Some of the following sentences have problems with sentence structure. If there is no error, write CORRECT. If there is an error in sentence structure, determine whether it is a fragment, a comma splice, or a run-on sentence. Then rewrite the sentence correctly. You many need to add some words.

1. When the girls left the dance at midnight.

   _____

2. Because our class had two tests to write on Monday.

   _____

3. The airplane rolled to a stop, we were glad to be home at last.

   _____

4. Huge waves crashed against the shoreline as the hurricane moved up the coast.

   _____

5. Studying for the last examination of the year.

   _____

6. The children raced across the playground; they did not hear their mother calling.

   _____

7. The movie ended we left the theatre.

   _____

8. Music and laughter filled the air we wished the night would never end.

   _____

   _____

C. Rewrite the following paragraph in your notebook, correcting each sentence error. Add capital letters and punctuation marks where needed.

During the 1860s. Almost all the Chinese who came to North America were from the province of Kwangtung in southeastern China. The capital of this region was Canton. One of the largest cities in the Orient. Canton was established about 214 B.C.E. by Shih Huang Ti. The emperor of China's Ch'in dynasty. Today the city is an industrial centre and a major Chinese port a railway links Canton to Hong Kong 120 km to the southeast.

Exercise 81 (Word Skills)

Homonyms: The Sound-Alikes

The word *homonym* comes from two Greek words: *homos*, meaning "same," and *onyma*, meaning "name." **Homonyms** are words that sound alike but have different spellings and meanings.

  EXAMPLE: bear   bare
            there   their   they're

In the box below are four pairs of homonyms that often cause problems.

Contractions		Possessive Pronouns	
it's	it is	**its**	its harness
they're	they are	**their**	their tools
who's	who is	**whose**	whose watch
you're	you are	**your**	your guitar

A. Cross out the incorrect homonym in each sentence. In your notebook write your own sentence using each crossed-out homonym correctly. Use your dictionary if necessary.

1. A red scarf would (complement, compliment) that outfit.

2. Colin certainly has a (flare, flair) for writing lyrics.

3. You'll find the (stationary, stationery) in the bottom drawer of the desk.

4. The earth's (mantel, mantle) is a thick layer of solid rock below the crust.

5. Being sent to the principal's office certainly didn't (faze, phase) Nick.

6. The (hail, hale) last week badly damaged the crops.

7. Parliament gave its (assent, ascent) to that bill on Tuesday.

8. My mother plans to (canvas, canvass) our neighbourhood for the Cancer Society this week.

9. The squirrel kept its (hoard, horde) of walnuts in an empty jam jar in our attic.

10. Injuries to the spinal (chord, cord) often cause paralysis.

B. Circle the correct words in each of the following sentences. In your notebook write sentences using the other homonyms correctly.

1. (They're, Their) not sure (who's, whose) key is required.

2. (It's, Its) far too stormy to be out in (they're, their) small boat.

3. (You're, Your) not the one that (they're, their) looking for.

4. Guess (who's, whose) coming to (they're, their) party.

Exercise 82 (Study Skills)

Using a Glossary

A **glossary** is a list of words and their meanings, often found at the back of a book. Words in a glossary are arranged in alphabetical order. The purpose of the glossary is to provide the reader with the vocabulary that is especially important for understanding the topics discussed in the book.

An effective study skill is to create your own glossaries for your school courses. Place a sheet of looseleaf paper at the beginning of your notebook for each subject. When your teacher introduces a new term, record it and its definition on this sheet along with the date of the class when you learned this term. Use drawings whenever possible to illustrate the concepts. Every Monday, look over your lists of terms, and test yourself on whether you can define each one. Keep these glossary pages in your notebook.

A. The following terms are taken from the glossaries of four books: a social studies text, a language arts text, a science text, and a mathematics text. Identify which textbook each term was found in, and tell how you know. If you are not sure, check the meanings in a dictionary.

1. photosynthesis _____

2. population distribution _____

3. probability _____

4. protagonist _____

B. Find a book—perhaps one of the textbooks you currently use—that contains a glossary. Write the title of the book below. Then browse through the glossary to get a sense of the words contained in it. In the space below copy three terms from the glossary that you feel are especially important for understanding the material in the book. Write definitions of each of these terms in your own words.

_____

_____

_____

_____

_____

_____

C. In your notebook create a glossary of twenty important terms found in this workbook. Remember to arrange your terms in alphabetical order and write your definitions in complete sentences.

UNIT
20

Exercise 83 (Word Skills)

Adding Suffixes to Words Ending in -e

Some root words change their spelling when suffixes are added.
1. Words that end in a silent -e usually keep the -e before a suffix beginning with a consonant.
    EXAMPLE: brave + ly = bravely   care + ful = careful

    However, this rule has four exceptions:

    argue + ment = argument   whole + ly = wholly
    true + ly = truly   nine + th = ninth

2. Words that end in a silent -e usually drop the -e before adding a suffix beginning with a vowel.
    EXAMPLE: fame + ous = famous   move + able = movable

    This rule has two exceptions:

    acre + age = acreage   notice + able = noticeable

3. Words such as *die*, *lie*, and *tie* change the *-ie* to *-y* before adding *-ing*.
    EXAMPLE: die + ing = dying   lie + ing = lying   tie + ing = tying

    Words ending in *-ce* or *-ge* usually drop the -e before a suffix beginning with *-e*, *-i*, or *-y*.
    EXAMPLE: spice + y = spicy   produce + ing = producing

Using these rules, write the word that is formed when the following root words and suffixes are joined.

EXAMPLE: life + less = *lifeless*

1. hope + ful = _____

2. hate + ing = _____

3. notice + able = _____

4. nine + ty = _____

5. excuse + able = _____

6. acknowledge + ment = _____

7. adventure + ous = _____

8. change + able = _____

9. collapse + ible = _____

10. excite + ment = _____

11. value + able = _____

12. safe + ly = _____

13. sincere + ly = _____

14. sense + ible = _____

15. encourage + ment = _____

16. nine + th = _____

17. scarce + est = _____

18. nerve + ous = _____

19. absolute + ly = _____

20. advertise + ment = _____

21. fortunate + ly = _____

22. improve + ment = _____

23. announce + ing = _____

24. tie + ing = _____

25. come + ing = _____

26. taste + less = _____

27. use + less = _____

28. believe + able = _____

Exercise 84 (Punctuation and Capitalization)

Using Commas with Parenthetical Expressions

Parenthetical expressions are words or phrases that writers and speakers use to make their ideas clear. The following are a few of the most common parenthetical expressions:

after all	for example	in my opinion	of course
as a matter of fact	for instance	in fact	on the contrary
by the way	generally speaking	moreover	therefore
consequently	however	nevertheless	

Parenthetical expressions are not necessary to the sentence and can be omitted without changing its meaning. To show this, they are separated from the rest of the sentence by commas. Parenthetical expressions may appear at the beginning, middle, or end of a sentence.

EXAMPLE: **Generally speaking**, the weather was quite cool while you were away.
On August 29, **in fact**, I thought we might have frost.
The overnight low was a few degrees above freezing, **however**.

Create sentences using the following phrases as parenthetical expressions. Check your work by reading the sentence without the parenthetical expression. The meaning of the sentence should not change. Add commas where needed.

1. by the way

_____

_____

2. I suppose

_____

_____

3. on the other hand

_____

_____

4. for example

_____

5. of course

_____

_____

6. however

_____

_____

UNIT 20

Communicating Skills 8 | **111**

Using Commas with Appositives

An **appositive** is a word or a group of words that renames or explains a noun in the sentence. Usually appositives come right after that noun.

EXAMPLE: Dr. Lee, **my dentist**, enjoys windsurfing on weekends.
Cape Spear, **the most easterly part of North America**, is near the entrance to St. John's Harbour in Newfoundland.

In these sentences, the boldface phrases are appositives because they give additional information about the nouns they follow. Notice that appositives are set off from the rest of the sentence by commas.

Write sentences using each of the following phrases as appositives. Be sure to punctuate each one correctly.

EXAMPLE: a river in South America ____The Amazon, a____ ____river in South America, contains more____ ____water than the Nile, the Mississippi,____ ____and the Yangtze Rivers combined.____

1. a good friend of mine _____

_____

_____

2. my favourite television program _____

_____

_____

3. our science teacher _____

_____

_____

4. the largest city in this area _____

_____

_____

5. the best book I've ever read _____

_____

_____

Exercise 86 (Sentence Construction)

Using Appositives to Combine Ideas

Appositives can often be used to join a number of short, choppy sentences into a longer, much smoother sentence.

> EXAMPLE: *Mount Logan is the highest peak in Canada. It is located in Kluane National Park. This park is a vast, mountainous region in the southwest corner of the Yukon Territory.*
>
> *Mount Logan, **Canada's highest peak**, is located in Kluane National Park, **a vast mountainous region in the southwest corner of the Yukon Territory**.*

Read each of the following pairs of sentences carefully. In each case, the second sentence gives further information about a noun in the first sentence. Combine each pair of sentences by making the second sentence into an appositive. Place the appositive directly after the noun it describes. Be sure to punctuate your sentences correctly.

1. Sir John A. Macdonald grew up in Kingston, Ontario. Macdonald was Canada's first prime minister.

   _____

   _____

2. Caroline Brunet won the Lou Marsh Award as Canada's top athlete of 1999. She is a native of Lac-Beauport, Quebec.

   _____

   _____

3. Kelowna has the third-busiest airport in British Columbia. Kelowna is a city on the east shore of Okanagan Lake.

   _____

   _____

4. David Pelletier and Jamie Sale won gold medals at the 2002 Winter Olympics. They are pairs figure skaters.

   _____

   _____

5. Digby has one of the world's largest scallop fleets. This town is on the west coast of Nova Scotia.

   _____

   _____

Punctuating Direct and Indirect Quotations

Writers know that dialogue—the words that people say—adds life and realism to writing. You can include the words that people say in two ways. A direct quotation gives the speaker's exact words.

EXAMPLE: *Josie replied, "I forgot to do my homework."*

An indirect quotation is a paraphrase of the person's words.

EXAMPLE: *Josie replied that she had forgotten to do her homework.*

When writing direct quotation, remember these rules:

1. Quotation marks (" ") indicate the beginning and end of direct quotations. They always come in pairs. Do not use quotation marks with indirect quotations.
2. To separate a direct quotation from the rest of the sentence, use a comma. If the quotation is at the beginning of the sentence, place the comma *inside* the second set of quotation marks.
3. If the quotation is not at the beginning of the sentence, the comma goes *before* the first set of quotation marks.
4. If the quotation is split into two parts with expressions such as *I said* or *the doctor replied*, be sure to use two sets of quotation marks.
5. When the quotation itself is a question or an exclamation, the question mark or exclamation point is placed inside the closing pair of quotation marks.
6. A direct quotation always begins with a capital letter. The first word in the second part of a divided quotation is capitalized *only* if it begins a new sentence.

EXAMPLE: *"I tried to stop," claimed the driver, "but the car just kept skidding."*
"I find that hard to believe," replied the traffic officer. "May I see your driver's licence?"

A. In each sentence, underline the exact words of the speaker and put in any punctuation marks that are needed. Draw three lines under any letters that should be capitalized.

EXAMPLE: After hearing my story the principal asked, "why did you do it?"

1. The clerk replied that set of stamps is quite expensive

2. Get that dog off the field shouted the umpire

3. Did you say to turn west on Harrison Avenue asked my father

4. Because I twisted my ankle replied Rachel I won't be at the practice tonight

5. Sold to the man in the back row shouted the auctioneer

6. What was that noise she whispered it sounded like it came from downstairs

7. My aunt said I've always liked dogs better than cats

Punctuating Direct and Indirect Quotations (continued)

B. Write interesting sentences of your own using the following directions.

1. A sentence containing a direct quotation and starting with My sister shouted.

_____

_____

2. A sentence containing a direct quotation and ending with the wrestler whispered.

_____

_____

3. A sentence containing a direct quotation interrupted with roared the monster.

_____

_____

4. A sentence containing a direct quotation and ending with asked the reporter.

_____

_____

5. A sentence containing a direct quotation and ending with screamed the bodyguard.

_____

_____

6. A sentence containing a direct quotation and starting with Suddenly the fire chief yelled.

_____

_____

7. A sentence containing a direct quotation interrupted with complained the coach.

_____

_____

8. A sentence containing a direct quotation and ending with gasped the alien creature.

_____

_____

_____

Exercise 88 (Word Skills)

Adding Suffixes to Words Ending in *-y*

1. Words ending in *-y* preceded by a consonant usually change the *-y* to *-i* before any suffix except one beginning with *-i*.

   EXAMPLE: cry + ed = cried   **but**   cry + ing = crying

   baby + ed = babied   **but**   baby + ish = babyish

   In English a few one-syllable words end in a consonant and the letter *y*. Dictionaries often give two spellings for these words when suffixes are added.

   EXAMPLE: dry + er (a machine that dries clothes) may be spelled *dryer* or *drier*

   fly + er (a person who flies) may be spelled *flyer* or *flier*

2. Words ending in *-y* preceded by a vowel usually keep the *-y* when a suffix is added.

   EXAMPLE: enjoy + able = enjoyable   pray + ed = prayed

   destroy + ing = destroying

   This rule has three exceptions:

   day + ly = daily   say + ed = said   lay + ed = laid

Join these word parts to make new words.

1. marry + ing = _____
2. rely + able = _____
3. buy + er = _____
4. pretty + est = _____
5. joy + ous = _____
6. satisfy + ed = _____
7. pay + ed = _____
8. apply + ed = _____
9. lonely + ness = _____
10. spry + est = _____
11. betray + ed = _____
12. enjoy + able = _____

13. envy + ous = _____
14. pray + ed = _____
15. try + ed = _____
16. try + ing = _____
17. magnify + ed = _____
18. multiply + ing = _____
19. leafy + er = _____
20. creepy + est = _____
21. fly + ing = _____
22. annoy + ed = _____
23. happy + est = _____
24. bury + ing = _____

Exercise 89 (Sentence Construction)

Writing Concise Sentences

Strong writing is **concise**, which means "brief and to the point." You can make your writing more concise in three ways:

1. Combine two or more short sentences to make one longer sentence.
2. Eliminate expressions such as *I think that*, *on account of*, and *due to the fact that*. These phrases do not add meaning to your prose; they slow down the communication of ideas.

    EXAMPLE: *It is my opinion that the Raptors will win the championship next year.*
    MORE CONCISE: *The Raptors will win the championship next year.*

3. Do not repeat an idea unnecessarily.

    EXAMPLE: *The wind often comes up after sunset when the sun goes down.*
    MORE CONCISE: *The wind often comes up after sunset.*

Rewrite the following sentences, omitting unnecessary words.

1. The point is that he kept repeating the same idea over and over again.

   _____

2. Because of the fact that gas prices have increased and got higher, my father has decided to take the bus to work at the office.

   _____

   _____

3. It's my opinion that despite the fact that it's raining, we should still play the game.

   _____

4. The strange object is hexagonal in shape and at this point in time is securely locked in our garage.

   _____

5. My mother loves to bring up controversial topics about which everyone has a different opinion.

   _____

   _____

6. When I was seven years of age, my parents took me to Storybook Gardens in the city of London, Ontario.

   _____

   _____

7. Sven flew to Moncton in a plane. His plane landed at 10 a.m. in the morning.

   _____

Exercise 90 (Composition Construction)

Narrative Writing: Dialogue

An effective way to make the characters in a narrative come alive is to let them talk to each other. The conversation written for a story, play, or motion picture is called **dialogue**. The words that people use to express themselves can reveal their age, education, personality, and character. Dialogue can also show the emotional state of the speakers and suggest conflicts.

When you write dialogue, be sure to punctuate correctly and follow these two rules:
1. Start a new paragraph each time the speaker changes.
2. When a speaker uses several sentences one after the other, enclose the entire paragraph in quotation marks, not each individual sentence.

A. The following conversation between Sam Carr, the owner of a drugstore, and Alfred Higgins, a boy who works for him, is from Morley Callaghan's story "All the Years of Her Life." The author uses conversation to give the reader insights into the personalities of Sam Carr and Alfred Higgins. Read the passage twice and explain what you learn about Sam and Alfred.

"Maybe you'd be good enough to take a few things out of your pocket and leave them here before you go," Sam Carr said.

"What things? What are you talking about?"

"You've got a compact and a lipstick and at least two tubes of toothpaste in your pockets, Alfred."

"What do you mean? Do you think I'm crazy?" Alfred blustered.

"Petty thieving, eh, Alfred?" Sam Carr said. "And maybe you'd be good enough to tell me how long this has been going on."

"This is the first time I ever took anything."

"So now you think you'll tell me a lie, eh? What kind of a sap do I look like, huh? I don't know what goes on in my own store, eh? I tell you you've been doing this pretty steady," Sam Carr said as he went over and stood behind the cash register.

_____

_____

_____

_____

_____

_____

_____

Narrative Writing: Dialogue (continued)

B. Read the following passage twice to get a sense of what the people in it are like. Then in your notebook rewrite the passage as a dialogue, using direct quotations to convey a strong sense of the people.

By the time she met Carlos, just before one o'clock Friday afternoon, Jessica was frantic. She asked if he'd seen Shane. Carlos casually mentioned he'd walked to school with Shane that morning but hadn't seen him since. Although he wasn't sure, he thought Shane was probably hanging out with his buddies in the computer lab. Jessica was upset because Shane had borrowed her English book the day before and hadn't returned it. She had spent the entire lunch hour looking for him. She knew she'd be late for science class next period if she took time to walk all the way down to the tech ed room. Besides, Shane might not even be there. He'd been known to skip school on Friday afternoon. On the other hand, if she didn't have her English book for last period, she'd probably get a detention. Jessica had never had a detention before. Trying to be helpful, Carlos said he would see Shane in gym next period and would ask him about the book then. He suggested they meet outside the cafeteria at the end of the next period. Jessica hurriedly agreed and dashed off to science class.

C. What do you think will happen when Carlos and Jessica meet outside the cafeteria? Continue the story to include the dialogue from this meeting.

_____

_____

_____

_____

_____

_____

_____

_____

_____

Exercise 91 (Punctuation and Capitalization)

Using Commas with Nouns in Direct Address

When you **address** someone, you speak directly to her or him. Sometimes you may call the person by name. At other times you may use the person's title, such as *Doctor* or *Your Honour*. These names or titles must be enclosed by commas if they interrupt the flow of the sentence.

EXAMPLE: *Did you know,* **Ranjit,** *that one-third of the people in New Brunswick speak French?*
When will you name the starting quarterback, **Coach?**

Rewrite these sentences using capitalization and punctuation where needed.

1. waiter may I please have a glass of water

   _____

2. yes krista st john's is the largest city in newfoundland and labrador

   _____

3. the town of minnedosa paul is about two hundred km northwest of winnipeg manitoba

   _____

   _____

4. are you sure this invention will work professor

   _____

5. you'll find what you're looking for in the top drawer sergeant

   _____

6. the apple pies on the kitchen table bernadette are for the bake sale at saint james church

   _____

   _____

7. are you flying to london on air canada british airways or american airlines dad

   _____

   _____

8. when will we be able to talk to lauren doctor

   _____

9. peter are you sure this is the right place

   _____

Exercise 92 (Grammar and Usage)

Pronouns: Making the Reference Clear

The word *ambiguous* means "having more than one possible meaning." The reference of a pronoun is ambiguous if the pronoun can refer to more than one word.

EXAMPLE: *The police officers chased the bank robbers until their car smashed into a lumber truck.*

In this sentence the pronoun "their" has two possible antecedents. Whose car crashed into the lumber truck—the police officers' or the bank robbers'?

REWORDED: *While chasing the bank robbers, the police officers' car crashed into a lumber truck.*

Sometimes the reference of the pronoun can be clarified by using quotation marks.

EXAMPLE: *Dustin asked his father if he could go to the hockey game.*
"May I go to the hockey game, Dad?" asked Dustin.

In each of the following sentences, the antecedent of the italicized pronoun is ambiguous. Rewrite each sentence to make the meaning clear.

1. There's a fly in your soup; do you want *it?*

   _____

2. Holly doesn't see Amber often since *she* moved to Fredericton.

   _____

   _____

3. Our car crashed into a fence, but *it* wasn't badly damaged.

   _____

4. His father won the lottery when *he* was sixteen.

   _____

5. First we took the shells off the walnuts; then we ate *them.*

   _____

6. When I dropped the cup on the saucer, *it* broke.

   _____

7. Amy watched Rebecca riding *her* horse.

   _____

8. Jason told Ricardo that *he* had the highest mark on the science test.

   _____

   _____

9. Take the goldfish out of the tanks and wash *them* thoroughly.

   _____

UNIT
23

Adding Suffixes to Words Ending in a Single Consonant

1. When a suffix beginning with a vowel is added to a one-syllable word ending in a single consonant, the final consonant is usually doubled.
   EXAMPLE: *bat + er = batter   red + ish = reddish   trap + er = trapper*

   However, when a word ends in -x, the final consonant is not doubled.
   EXAMPLE: *mix + ed = mixed   tax + ing = taxing   six + th = sixth*

2. The final consonant in one-syllable words is not doubled if the following are true:
   a. the suffix begins with a consonant.
      EXAMPLE: *cup + ful = cupful   sad + ly = sadly   mad + ness = madness*
   b. there are two vowels before the final consonant.
      EXAMPLE: *seal + ed = sealed   jail + er = jailer   soak + ing = soaking*
   c. the word ends in more than one consonant.
      EXAMPLE: *third + ly = thirdly   hard + est = hardest   churn + ed = churned*

3. Words of more than one syllable ending in a single consonant other than -x or -w usually double the final consonant if the suffix begins with a vowel.
   EXAMPLES: *oc**cur** + ed = occurred   ad**mit** + ance = admittance*

   There are some exceptions, so check your dictionary if you are unsure.

A. Join these one-syllable word parts to make new words.

1. soak + ed = _____
2. trim + er = _____
3. coat + less = _____
4. shop + er = _____
5. stop + ing = _____
6. drug + ist = _____
7. shed + ing = _____

8. heat + ed = _____
9. flat + est = _____
10. mat + ed = _____
11. ship + er = _____
12. ship + ment = _____
13. heap + ing = _____
14. dim + est = _____

B. Join these two-syllable words to suffixes to make new words.

1. omit + ed = _____
2. yellow + er = _____
3. forbid + en = _____
4. gallop + ed = _____
5. relax + ed = _____
6. begin + er = _____
7. total + ed = _____

8. equip + ing = _____
9. equip + ment = _____
10. permit + ed = _____
11. lonely + ness = _____
12. occur + ed = _____
13. rebel + ion = _____
14. prepare + ed = _____

Exercise 94 (Punctuation and Capitalization)

Writing Titles

When writing titles and subtitles, capitalize the first, last, and major words—nouns, verbs, adjectives, and adverbs. Some titles require different forms of punctuation.

1. The titles of books, plays, newspapers, magazines, longer poems, pamphlets, films, television and radio programs, recordings, works of visual art, musical compositions, comic strips, and software should be italicized. When you write by hand, they should be underlined to indicate italics.

2. Quotation marks are used to set off titles of newspaper and magazine articles, short stories, poems, songs, episodes of television and radio programs, and chapters or subdivisions of books.

   EXAMPLE: Our class read Margaret Atwood's short story "The Man from Mars," found in the anthology *Classic Short Fiction.*

Proofread these sentences, using proofreading marks to show all necessary capital letters and punctuation marks. Underline to indicate italics.

1. rita macneil a singer from big pond nova scotia is well known for songs such as flying on your own and working man

2. canadian singer and songwriter gordon lightfoot was canadas most popular male vocalist during the 1970s three of his best known songs are early morning rain did she mention my name and the wreck of the edmund fitzgerald

3. susan aglukark is a canadian inuit singer and songwriter her 1999 cd included songs such as bridge of dreams gathering place and never be the same she was born in churchill manitoba

4. for next english period be sure to read chapter five expressing an opinion

5. our teacher ms hinkson asked the class to memorize alden nowlans poem the bull moose alden nowlan was born near windsor nova scotia and one of his books bread wine and salt won the governor generals award in 1967

6. sharon pollocks play the komagata maru incident is based on canadas handling of the arrival of a boatload of sikh immigrants in 1914

7. coca: an ancient herb turns deadly an article by peter t. white in the january 1989 edition of national geographic was very useful in writing this report

Exercise 95 (Punctuation and Capitalization)

Further Uses of Quotation Marks

> Use quotation marks to identify words used as words. If you are using a word-processing program, you can italicize these words.
>
> *EXAMPLE:* Students sometimes confuse the words "their" and "there."
>
> Use single quotation marks to enclose a quotation that appears within a quotation.
>
> *EXAMPLE:* Mayor Deborah Ellsworth replied, "The commissioner's promise that there would be 'no significant increase in utility costs' was unrealistic."

Copy the following sentences in the blanks, adding all necessary capital letters and punctuation. Underline to indicate italics.

1. The lawyer assured us that the word trespass would not appear on the report.

2. Janice asked did you read the article in Runners Weekly Magazine called run for your life?

3. The teacher explained that whether is not the word to use when discussing atmospheric conditions.

4. I heard Rafe say take exit four when he gave you directions said Stephanie.

5. Flaunt and flout do not mean the same thing.

6. You should not use the preposition between when you are discussing more than two people or items.

7. Ben asked Carol was it you who taped the word skaterboy on my back?

8. The in sign fell off the entrance door.

Exercise 96 (Composition Construction)

Introducing an Essay

An **essay** is a multiparagraph discussion of a topic that presents its information in the manner that is best suited to its purpose. For example, there are narrative essays, descriptive essays, comparative essays, cause-and-effect essays, essays of classification, problem–solution essays, and many more. Although there are many different kinds of essays, all of them include an introduction that must do two things: catch the reader's attention and identify the topic that will be discussed.

Assume that you have researched teen bullying and have discovered several important ideas, such as why some individuals begin bullying, why many teens are reluctant to reveal that they are victims of bullying, and important steps that individuals and community members can take to reduce incidents of bullying. You can introduce your topic in many ways that will catch a reader's interest.

1. Begin with an action related to the main idea:
    EXAMPLE: *The shy fourteen-year-old tried to ignore the taunts that began the moment she stepped off the bus, but she could not ignore the hand that shoved her forward into the brick wall. And Canadians cannot ignore the fact that bullying is on the rise in many schools....*

2. Begin with dialogue in which people (real or imagined) discuss the issue.
    EXAMPLE: *"Just don't say anything and maybe he'll leave us alone," Jacob whispered.*
    "Yeah, like that worked last time," Kyle muttered.
    "Hey, maggots!" came the voice they both dreaded. It was starting again.
    Bullying is a problem faced by many young people in Canadian schools....

3. Begin with a comment made by a respected authority.
    EXAMPLE: *"Bullying is often the unseen crime," explained Sheryl Goldstein, principal of Everwood Junior High School. "And it is only getting worse."*
    Ms. Goldstein is not the only one who believes that incidents of bullying are on the rise....

4. Put a face on your subject by describing a person who represents people associated with the topic.
    EXAMPLE: *Kari Rudniki was bullied throughout elementary school. When it continued in junior high, her constant fear and anxiety led to bleeding ulcers and two suicide attempts. People like Kari are...*

5. Begin with the statement of a problem.
    EXAMPLE: *Schoolyard bullying does not end when children leave the elementary grades and move on to junior high and high schools. For many students, it only gets worse.*

In Activity A in Exercise 66, you developed a list of issues about which you feel strongly. Choose one of these issues and, in your notebook, write three different introductions for an essay on that topic. (You do not have to write the essay.) Then decide which introduction you like best and tell why.

Commonly Confused Words: Part 1

Many words in English are often used incorrectly because they look and sound somewhat alike. It is important to identify the words that you frequently misuse so that you can learn to use them correctly.

A. The numbered sets of words in the box match the numbered groups of sentences. Read each group of sentences carefully. Decide which word will fit in each blank. (With some of the verbs, you may have to use the past tense. Use your dictionary if necessary.)

1. accept, except	4. angle, angel	7. conscious, conscience
2. advice, advise	5. bisect, dissect	8. desert, dessert
3. affect, effect	6. breath, breathe	9. decent, descent, dissent

1. Our science teacher will not _____ late assignments.

   All of the girls went swimming _____ Janine.

2. I would _____ you to read the directions carefully.

   What _____ did the coach give Tak before the race?

3. What will be the _____ of the new rule?

   Will the new rule _____ you?

4. When she wants something, my sister behaves like an _____.

   Be sure to measure the _____ carefully before you cut the wood.

5. Do you know how to _____ an angle?

   In biology my sister had to _____ a frog.

6. "Let me catch my _____" she gasped.

   Can you _____ normally now?

7. The old man remained _____ for half an hour.

   My _____ won't let me do that.

8. After seven days in the _____ they finally found water.

   My father often makes plum pie for _____.

9. The _____ into the cave is steep and dangerous.

   Most of the class wanted to play baseball, but four boys _____.

   The _____ thing to do would be to apologize.

Commonly Confused Words: Part 1 (continued)

B. In your notebook write sentences of your own, using each of the words in the box in Activity A.

C. Which of the words in the box in Activity A usually cause problems for you? Invent memory tricks that will help you remember their use. (For example, *affect* and *accept* both begin with *a* and are *action words*—verbs. Therefore, use these when you intend an action.)

_____

_____

_____

_____

_____

_____

_____

_____

D. Sometimes, misusing these words can create amusing errors; for example, *The child wanted to be an angle in the school play.* Create two amusing errors and explain the humour in each.

_____

_____

_____

_____

_____

_____

_____

E. In your notebook make a personal word list containing other words that you misuse. Add at least one word to this list every week, and write sentences using each word correctly. Refer to this word list frequently so you will not misuse these words in the future.

Exercise 98 (Composition Construction)

Writing the Thesis Statement

You have learned that a topic sentence identifies the subject of a paragraph. A thesis statement is a sentence that identifies the subject of an essay. Thesis statements appear in the introduction of an essay and are especially helpful when a writer plans to discuss several related ideas, because they state—or imply—the subtopics that will be examined in the paragraphs that follow. A thesis statement helps prepare the reader for what is to come.

EXAMPLE: *Bang! Car after car hits the huge hole on Commercial Street, rattling drivers' spines and dislodging loose parts from vehicles that are unable to avoid it. Middlewood residents have begun calling it "the mother of all potholes," complaining that recent attempts by highway crews to repair it have only made it worse. And it is only one of several such holes that have begun to appear along this busy stretch of road since the exit ramp from Highway 109 was completed last fall.* **Town officials need to survey traffic patterns and explore alternate throughway routes to prevent excessive road wear, decrease maintenance costs, and avoid creating road hazards that may result in personal injury and legal action.**

A. In the blanks below identify the subtopics that will be discussed in the essay that will follow the introduction shown above.

_____

_____

_____

_____

_____

_____

B. In the activity in Exercise 96, you wrote three introductions for an essay on an issue about which you feel strongly. What subtopics could such an essay include? Choose one of your introductions and rewrite it below, this time including a thesis statement that identifies the various subtopics that could appear in your essay.

_____

_____

_____

_____

_____

_____

Exercise 99 (Study Skills)

Locating Information in a Book

Finding information in a book is easier when you use the tools the book provides for you. Most reference books or textbooks include one or more features that enable readers to locate information quickly, such as a table of contents, an index, headings, graphic elements, and captions.

A. In the blanks below explain what each feature is and tell how it enables readers to locate information quickly.

1. table of contents _____

_____

2. index _____

_____

3. headings _____

_____

4. different fonts _____

_____

5. graphic elements (charts, diagrams, pictures) _____

_____

6. captions _____

_____

B. When is it more useful to turn to the table of contents and when is it more useful to use the index?

_____

C. Choose a reference book or textbook approved by your teacher and identify which of the features listed in Activity A are found in that book.

_____

D. Choose a specific topic in your reference book or textbook that is identified by at least three of the features listed in Activity A. In your notebook tell which features identify it and how.

E. Assume that you have to find information on solar eclipses in a science book. In your notebook explain how you would find this information, telling what you would do first, what you would do next, and so on.

Exercise 100 (Punctuation and Capitalization)

Using the Ellipsis

An **ellipsis** is a form of punctuation consisting of three dots (...). Writers use ellipses (plural of ellipsis) for two main purposes:

1. An ellipsis shows readers that one or more words of a quotation have been omitted. However, the writer must be careful not to change the intent of the quoted passage. For example, if a reporter wants to include a statement by the mayor about the bus strike but does not want to include every word, the reporter will use an ellipsis to show that something has been omitted.

   EXAMPLE: *On Thursday, Mayor Leblanc explained that "the bus strike will not be allowed to interfere with the arrival of sports teams, judges, and spectators who are attending the city's anniversary games."*

   USING THE ELLIPSIS: *On Thursday, Mayor Leblanc explained that "the bus strike will not be allowed to interfere with the ... city's anniversary games."*

2. In narrative writing, an ellipsis within dialogue gives readers the impression that the speaker is struggling to find the right words to say. An ellipsis at the end of dialogue gives the impression that the speaker's voice had trailed off.

   EXAMPLE: *Julie looked at the teacher and said, "I ... well, you see, Ms. Collins, I meant to do my homework last night, but ... uh ... I kind of forgot ..."*

A. In the blanks below copy the following passage, leaving out some of the unnecessary words but without changing the intent of the passage. Remember to use an ellipsis whenever you omit words.

> Alejandro told the police officer, "I was walking home through the park last night after leaving my girlfriend's place around 9:30, and I had just entered the street when I saw two masked men run out of the bakery on Pine Avenue. The owner, Mr. Buhagiar, came running out after them, and he was shouting for the police. I could see that his shoulder was bleeding. I was carrying some school stuff, and I dropped my books and ran to help him."

_____

_____

_____

_____

_____

_____

_____

B. Yesterday, Jeremy told Elise that he was too busy to take her to the cinema last night, but a friend told her that he saw Jeremy at the cinema last night with Angela. Elise has just seen Jeremy in the hallway at school. In your notebook write a dialogue between the two that includes at least three ellipses.

Commonly Confused Words: Part 2

In Exercise 97, you reviewed several pairs of words that create problems for many students. The following are more words that need to be handled carefully.

A. The numbered pairs of words in the box match the numbered groups of sentences. Read each of the sentences carefully. Decide which word will fit in each blank. (With some of the verbs, you may have to use the past tense. Use your dictionary if necessary.)

1. emigrate, immigrate	4. moral, morale
2. envelop, envelope	5. whether, weather
3. insight, incite	6. access, excess

1. When did your parents _____ to Canada from Hong Kong?

   Did your grandfather _____ from Germany in 1947?

2. The _____ was torn before it was delivered.

   Every fall heavy fogs often _____ the village.

3. Carl had a good _____ into how the machine worked.

   The speaker tried to _____ the troops to rebel.

4. Do you understand the _____ of that fable?

   The captain was pleased with the _____ of his crew.

5. The _____ yesterday was cloudy with showers.

   _____ or not we win the final game, our team will still be in first place.

6. Cut off the _____ fabric and save it for other uses.

   Do you have _____ to a public library?

B. Here are more word pairs that are often confused. Write sentences in your notebook using each of these words correctly.

allude – elude	later – latter	tack – tact
bizarre – bazaar	loose – lose	taunt – taut
diary – dairy	persecute – prosecute	than – then
eminent – imminent	proceed – precede	verses – versus
ensure – insure	statue – statute	cease – seize

Exercise 102 (Composition Construction)

Writing Developmental Paragraphs

You learned in Exercise 96 that the introductory paragraph of an essay should catch the reader's attention, introduce the essay's main idea, and let the reader know where the essay is going. The middle paragraphs are called developmental paragraphs because they develop and support the main idea of the essay. Each developmental paragraph should deal with one part of the main idea.

A. Here is the introductory paragraph for an essay called "All Kinds of Feet." In the blank below tell what the main idea of the essay will be.

Like most people, you probably use your feet for standing, running, and walking. By contrast, birds' feet perform an amazing assortment of tasks such as paddling around pools, gripping branches, and seizing snakes and small mammals. Birds' feet come in more types and sizes than you could imagine.

_____

B. Read the essay's three developmental paragraphs and, after each, identify the main idea of the paragraph and the details that the writer has used to develop that idea.

I. Many birds use their feet for gripping things. Perching birds, for example, have three toes pointing forward and one backward so they can wrap their toes around a limb and hold on firmly. Climbing birds, such as woodpeckers and parrots, have two toes pointing forward and two backward. The hind toes dig in when ascending, letting these birds cling securely to tree trunks.

_____

_____

_____

II. The toes of most water birds, such as ducks, geese, and gulls, are connected by broad webs of tough leathery skin, transforming their feet into superb paddles. With ducks and gulls, the web connects only the three forward toes. Gannets, cormorants, and pelicans, however, have all four toes joined by webs, increasing their paddling area by nearly one-third. A few water birds, including coots and grebes, have flaps of skin along the toes instead of webbed feet.

_____

_____

_____

_____

Writing Developmental Paragraphs (continued)

III. Birds of prey such as hawks, eagles, vultures, and owls seize their food with their feet. These powerful birds catch, crush, and carry off their victims with sharp, vise-like talons. Watching the ground intently from high overhead, these skilled hunters swoop down on prey with lightning speed. When they strike their target, their talons automatically clench. Fish-eating birds, such as ospreys, are sometimes pulled under water and drowned when they lock onto too large a fish and cannot release their grip in time.

_____

_____

_____

C. Assume that your English teacher has asked you to write a research essay on an unusual animal. You have decided to write about porcupines, and you have narrowed your topic to the porcupine's *appearance*. Below is the point-form information you have collected on your topic. Use this information to write the developmental paragraphs that will appear in your essay. Wherever possible, use transitional expressions to move smoothly from one idea to another.

I. Feet
- walks flat-footed, like a bear
- is pigeon-toed and bowlegged
- four toes on front feet, five on hind feet
- long curved black claws on toes
- claws make them excellent climbers
- claws hold food when the animal sits up

II. Tail
- quite short and thick
- braces itself with its tail when sitting
- used for balance when moving along branches
- stiff bristles on underside—a useful prop when climbing
- guides the porcupine when backing down trees
- swings its tail from side to side, strikes out at attacker

III. Quills
- cover back and sides from the eyes to near the end of the tail
- most have about 30 000 quills
- usually not more than seventeen centimetres long
- lie flat pointing toward the tail when the animal is calm and undisturbed
- quickly raised if danger is near
- cannot actually throw its quills
- quills come out easily into the victim's flesh
- small hooks on quill tips force them deeper and deeper

Exercise 103 (Composition Construction)

Writing the Concluding Paragraph

The purpose of an essay's concluding paragraph is to pull together the writer's ideas and end the essay smoothly. Be careful not to introduce new ideas in a concluding paragraph. When the content of an essay is straightforward, the concluding paragraph may be brief. However, when an essay presents several complex ideas, the writer may choose to summarize the main points that have been mentioned.

A. In Exercise 102, you read the introductory and developmental paragraphs of the essay titled "All Kinds of Feet." Below is the essay's concluding paragraph. Read it and tell whether it is an effective conclusion. Why or why not?

The more you study birds' feet, the more remarkable they seem. Every small detail, such as the shape of the nails, the number of joints, and the different ways they connect, has a definite purpose. By examining a bird's feet you can learn much about how that bird lives.

_____

_____

_____

_____

B. Read the developmental paragraphs you wrote in Activity C in Exercise 102. In the blanks below write a concluding paragraph for your essay on porcupines. Be sure not to introduce any new ideas. Try to restate briefly, in an interesting way, what the essay has been about.

_____

_____

_____

_____

_____

_____

_____

_____

A. Circle the correct words in the following sentences.

1. (They're, Their) wondering (who's, whose) driving to the soccer game.

2. Was it (your, you're) dog that cut (it's, its) front left paw on a broken bottle?

B. Correctly spell the word that is formed when the following root words and suffixes are joined.

1. hope + ful = _____

2. lonely + ness = _____

3. shed + ing = _____

4. try + ed = _____

5. change + able = _____

6. hot + est = _____

C. Circle the correct word in each set of parentheses.

1. Terri offered to (accept, except) responsibility for the damage.

2. My parents gave me (advice, advise) about applying for an after-school job.

3. This cough medicine can (affect, effect) a person's driving.

4. What did the restaurant serve for (desert, dessert)?

5. You might find it hard to (breath, breathe) when air pollution levels are high.

D. Use proofreading marks to indicate all necessary capital letters and punctuation.

1. catherine oliver my mothers older sister wrote a novel called summer of hope

2. jared asked the teacher do we have to do all four exercises sir

3. as a matter of fact the game was delayed

4. class please read the poem the road not taken instructed the teacher

E. Rewrite each sentence to avoid ambiguous pronoun reference.

1. The plate hit my foot, but it didn't break.

_____

2. Andrew doesn't see Jason often since he entered high school.

_____

3. We peeled the shells off the hard-boiled eggs, and then we ate them.

_____

4. The goalie kicked it down the field.

_____

Review (continued)

F. Read the following sentences and decide whether they are written correctly or if they contain errors in sentence structure. If a sentence is correct, put a check mark in the blank. If a sentence is a fragment, a comma splice, or a run-on sentence, write F or CS or RO in the blank.

_____ 1. Even after the bus had rolled to a stop in the school parking lot.

_____ 2. Because the girls lost the last game, they did not advance to regional playoffs.

_____ 3. A dog began barking furiously, Jake turned and walked away from the house.

_____ 4. Lee has been exercising regularly for months she often runs four kilometres before school.

_____ 5. Dancing with the captain of the girls' volleyball team.

G. Rewrite the following sentences, omitting unnecessary words.

1. He refused to be quiet and continued talking.

_____

2. In my opinion, I think we need to present our complaint to the student council.

_____

3. At this point in time, gas prices are still rising rapidly.

_____

H. In the blanks answer these questions about an essay.

1. Describe five ways a writer can introduce an essay's topic.

_____

_____

_____

_____

_____

2. When is a thesis statement especially helpful in an essay?

_____

3. Explain the purpose of an essay's concluding paragraph.

_____

afraid	anxious, cowardly, horrified, fearful, frightened, nervous, scared, terrified, troubled, uneasy
angry	annoyed, aroused, cross, enraged, furious, in a rage, inflamed, infuriated, irate, peeved
ask	demand, inquire, question, quiz, request
bad	awful, evil, horrible, naughty, rotten, spoiled, unfavourable, unpleasant, wicked, wrong
beautiful	attractive, charming, dazzling, desirable, elegant, gorgeous, handsome, lovely, magnificent, pretty, sparkling, splendid, stunning
begin	commence, inaugurate, launch, start
big	colossal, enormous, gigantic, great, huge, immense, jumbo, large, mammoth, massive, titanic, vast
brave	bold, courageous, daring, fearless, gallant, heroic, unafraid, valiant
break	burst, crack, crush, damage, destroy, shatter, smash, split, wreck
bright	brilliant, colourful, dazzling, gleaming, glittering, glowing, shimmering, shiny, sparkling
call	bellow, cry, roar, scream, whisper, yell
catch	capture, grab, hook, rope, snare, snatch
cool	bitter, chilly, cold, freezing, frigid, frosty, ice cold, icy, unheated, wintry
cry	bawl, bellow, exclaim, howl, roar, scream, shout, sob, wail, weep, yell
cut	carve, chop, clip, saw, slash, slice, snip
dark	black, dim, dismal, dreary, gloomy, murky, shadowy, sunless
delicious	appetizing, enjoyable, juicy, luscious, scrumptious, succulent, tasty
dirty	dingy, dusty, filthy, grimy, messy, smudged, soiled, unwashed
dull	boring, dreary, humdrum, tedious, tiring, uninteresting
eat	bite, chew, crunch, devour, feast on, gnaw, gobble, graze, grind, gulp, munch, nibble, swallow
fall	collapse, dive, drop, plunge, sink, topple, tumble
fast	fleet, hasty, prompt, quick, rapid, speedy, swift
fat	chubby, obese, overweight, plump, pudgy, stout

full	crammed, crowded, heaping, jammed, loaded, overflowing, packed, stuffed
get	acquire, collect, earn, find, gather, obtain
good	agreeable, excellent, fine, first-rate, marvellous, pleasant, reliable, satisfactory, splendid, superb, superior, well-behaved, wonderful, trustworthy
happy	cheerful, contented, delighted, glad, jolly, joyful, jubilant, merry, overjoyed, pleased, satisfied.
hate	abhor, despise, detest, disapprove, dislike, loathe
hit	collide, crash into, pound, punch, run into, slam into, smash into, strike
hot	baked, boiling, burning, fiery, roasting, scalded, scorched, sizzling, steaming, sunny, tropical, warm
hurry	accelerate, bustle, dart, dash, flash, hasten, hustle, race, run, rush, speed, zip, zoom
important	essential, famous, indispensable, influential, necessary, outstanding, prominent, significant, substantial, valuable, well-known
interesting	absorbing, appealing, amusing, arousing, attractive, engrossing, entertaining, enthralling, exciting, fascinating, gripping, intriguing, spellbinding, thrilling
kind	considerate, friendly, generous, gentle, helpful, pleasant, thoughtful, warm-hearted
little	dwarfish, miniature, minute, pigmy, small, tiny, wee
look	explore, gape, gawk, glance, glare, glimpse, hunt, inspect, observe, peek, peep, peer, search for, stare, study, watch
mad	angry, annoyed, cross, disagreeable, enraged, furious, raging
make	assemble, build, construct, create, develop, fashion, invent, manufacture, produce
move	amble, bound, climb, crawl, creep, dart, dash, gallop, hobble, jog, paddle, race, ride, run, rush, saunter, scamper, scramble, scurry, shuffle, slide, slither, stagger, streak, stride, swagger, tear, toddle, trot, waddle, walk
new	current, modern, recent, unused
old	aged, ancient, antique, elderly, feeble
right	accurate, correct, exact, perfect, true
sad	dejected, depressed, gloomy, miserable, sorrowful, sorry, unhappy

say	admit, announce, argue, assert, boast, chat, claim, comment, complaint, continue, discuss, explain, express, grumble, growl, insist, mention, mumble, mutter, note, order, promise, recall, remark, reply, snap, suggest, thunder, urge, whisper, yell
show	demonstrate, disclose, explain, guide, point out, teach
slowly	gradually, lazily, leisurely, sluggishly, unhurriedly
smart	bright, brilliant, clever, intellectual, intelligent, wise
stop	block, cease, conclude, discontinue, end, halt, prevent
strange	astonishing, extraordinary, fantastic, odd, peculiar, queer, unusual, weird
strong	forceful, mighty, muscular, powerful, rugged, sturdy, tough
take	capture, carry off, grab, kidnap, obtain, pick up, seize, snap up, snatch
thin	lean, scrawny, skinny, slender, slim
true	accurate, actual, authentic, correct, exact, genuine, real, right
ugly	hideous, repulsive, unattractive, unsightly
unhappy	cheerless, dejected, depressed, discontented, discouraged, gloomy, heart-broken, miserable, sad, sorrowful
walk	file, hike, limp, march, pace, prance, stagger, stalk, stamp, stride, stroll, strut, stumble, tiptoe, trudge, waddle
wet	damp, drenched, humid, moist, rainy, soaked, sodden, soggy, watery
wonderful	amazing, delightful, enjoyable, fabulous, fantastic, marvellous, spectacular, superb
worried	agitated, anxious, concerned, disturbed, troubled, upset
wrong	false, inaccurate, incorrect, unsuitable, untrue

INDEX

Active voice, 55
Adjectives, 71, 82
Adverb clauses, 76
Adverbs, 75, 82
Alliteration, 13
Antecedents, 88, 98, 121
Antonyms, 26, 86
Apostrophes, 89, 92
Appositives, 112, 113
Audience, 1, 21
Business letters, 56
Canadian spelling, 59
Capitalization, 7
Captions, 129
Clauses
    adjective, 93
    adverb, 76
    definition of, 24
    dependent, 24, 64
    independent, 24, 64
    main, 24, 64
    nonrestrictive, 94
    restrictive, 94
    subordinate, 24, 64
Colons, 58
Comma splices, 106
Commas
    with addresses, 10
    with appositives, 112
    with dates, 10
    in direct address, 120
    with parenthetical expressions, 111
    with a series, 9
Comparative form, 82
Comparison, 82
Compounds
    nouns, 6
    predicates, 32
    sentences, 28
    subjects, 32, 46
Concept map, 38
Concise writing, 117
Concluding paragraphs, 134
Confusing words, 126, 131
Conjunctions, 27, 64
Connotation, 30
Contractions, 92
Dashes, 40

Denotation, 30
Descriptive writing, 1, 30
Developmental paragraphs, 132
Dialogue, 118
Dictionary skills, 60
Direct address, commas and, 120
Directions, writing, 74
Editing, 66
Ellipses, 130
Essay, 125
Etymology, 72
Examples, explaining with, 77
Expository writing, 1, 74, 77, 79
Figurative language, 29
Formal language, 4
Glossaries, 109
Graphic elements, 129
Graphic organizers, 38
Greek roots, 80
Headings, 129
Homonyms, 108
Hyphens, 62
Indexes, 129
Informal language, 4
Information, locating, 129
Inquiry chart, 38
Internet, 35
Introductory paragraphs, 125
Inverted sentence order, 18
Journaling, 2
Language levels, 4
Latin roots, 72
Lie and *Lay*, 68
Limiting a topic, 22
Literary devices, 13, 29
Metaphor, 29
Narrative writing, 1, 118
Narrowing a topic, 22
Natural sentence order, 18
News writing, 14
Nonstandard language, 4
Nouns
    common, 6

    compound, 6
    definition of, 5
    general, 25
    plural, 8
    possessive, 89
    proper, 6
    singular, 8
    specific, 25
    types of, 6
Number prefixes, 90
Objects, 19
Onomatopoeia, 13
Order of ideas, 43
Parentheses, 40
Passive voice, 55
Person, 11, 12
Personal journaling, 2
Personification, 29
Persuasive writing, 1, 84
Phrases, 24, 96
Positive form, 82
Predicates, 17, 32
Prefixes, 86, 90
Prepositional phrases, 96, 102
Prepositions, 96
Pronouns
    antecedents and, 88, 98, 121
    case of, 100
    definition of, 88
    indefinite, 98
    objective case, 100
    person, 11
    relative, 93, 94
    subjective case, 100
Proofreading, 78
Purpose, 1, 21
Quotation marks, 114, 123, 124
Reasons, explaining with, 79
Research, 35, 36
Roots
    Greek, 80
    Latin, 72
    other languages, 83
    prefixes and, 86
    suffixes and, 99
Semicolons, 58
Sentences
    combining, 102, 113
    comma splices and,

    106
    complex, 64, 93
    compound, 28
    fragments, 106
    order of, 18
    parts of, 16, 17
    problems with, 106
    run-on, 106
    simple, 28
Simile, 29
Software, 63, 105
Spell-checkers, 63
Spelling, Canadian, 59
Split sentence order, 18
Subject-verb agreement, 41, 42, 46, 48, 50
Subjects
    complete, 16
    compound, 32, 46
    definition of, 16
    position of, 18, 48
    simple, 16
Suffixes, 99, 110, 115, 122
Superlative form, 82
Synonyms, 26
Tables of contents, 129
Tenses, 52
Thesaurus, 26, 105
Thesis statements, 128
Titles, capitalization and punctuation of, 123
Topic sentences, 44, 45
Topics, 21, 22
Transitional expressions, 54
Verbs
    agreement with subject, 41, 42
    auxiliary, 51
    choosing, 53
    definition of, 17
    helping, 51
    intransitive, 19
    linking, 20
    main, 51
    principal, 51
    state of being, 20
    tenses of, 52
    transitive, 19
    voice of, 55
Voice, 55